THIS STORY CONTAINS content that might be troubling to some readers, such as: sexual harassment, panic attacks, feelings of grief, trauma, violence, substance abuse and bullying. Please be mindful of these and other possible triggers, and seek assistance if needed from the resources at the end of the book.

# The Butterfly Sanctuary

Written by Georgia Peterson

*To my parents. You gave me everything and asked for nothing. To my friends who were excited with me and motivated me to continue. And lastly to you, my readers! I can't express how much I appreciate every single one of you for reading my FIRST book!*

# 1.

## Jane

Present day,

Jane runs with all her power towards the woods. She hears her attacker scream with anguish, then he hollers to his boys to begin the chase. Obediently, a rush of footsteps thunder behind her. She turns her head to the left, hair flying across her face, to glance at her pursuers. They're gaining on her.

Her chest tightens, chills rushing over her like a tsunami, and her heartbeat accelerates with every step. She pumps her legs harder, pushing herself, high on adrenaline. Her throat throbs, choking on her breath and rejecting it. Jane's whole body feels like it's in survival mode. A burning sensation traveling through her. The sudden adrenaline burst has rattled her. She can't continue for much longer.

Just as she's about to give up and accept her fate, her foot catches in a root, making her ankle tear apart. She screams, and she tumbles into a forward roll; arms and legs in a flurry.

The searing pain is like nothing she's ever felt before. Finally, the tumbling comes to an end. She lays flat on her back, the air kicked out of her. Every part of her aches. She turns onto her stomach, grunting as she drags herself beneath some undergrowth before her pursuers spot her.

Excruciating pain rumbles through her ankle. She screams out, then smacks her hand over her mouth, forcing herself not to make another sound. Tears escape her eyes; her heart feeling like it's going to beat out of her chest.

Footsteps come close by, the attacker straining his eyes to spy his lost possession. She knows he will have heard her scream; will know she's fallen and now lies vulnerable.

He sighs, giving up on searching in the dark. She hears him twist around on his heels, heading back to the campsite, not knowing that if he had just looked down, he would've seen a path flattened into the undergrowth, leading to his sweet, sweet Jane.

Jane peers up through that same undergrowth and can just make him out in the dim light. She holds her breath and tries to stop her shaking. She watches him leave. He yells out to the boys to head back to the campsite. If he'd just looked properly, he probably would've seen her, but he's always been lazy.

She raises her head to have a peep at her ankle and almost faints. It's facing the wrong direction. Thumping her fists on the ground on either side of her, she curses her life. She wants to scream out with anger but instead, sighs heavily, letting her head drop. Exhaustion finally hits and takes its grip on her. Accepting it, Jane takes hold of it. No more struggling, she thinks. She lets it whisk her away, the cold erupting through her body, laying her down before plunging her into darkness.

2.


Jane

Nine months earlier,

Butterflies swirled in her stomach as she put on her clothes. The first day of her last year at high school; she wasn't sure how to feel.

She wished she went to a private school, but since it was just her and her mom, they could only afford a public school. Jane didn't mind anyway; she didn't want to make her mom feel guilty or like she had to pick up more shifts at the hospital. Things were already pretty bad, considering she only really saw her mom at dinner times. Sometimes it would only be for a few minutes, and the whole time her mom would be scoffing down her food before she went to sleep for a couple of hours or went back to the hospital for the night shift. Jane was used to this but for some reason this morning felt different.

Jane came out of her room to the smell of syrup. An image of pancakes popped into her mind and she swiftly pushed it away, refusing to get her hopes up. Tugging on her skirt, she rounded the corner to witness her mom flipping pancakes. Her mom. Her mother was making her breakfast.

She's here for once, Jane thought.

Jane sat down at the table, afraid to say a word just in case it was a dream and it would all disappear. The last time her mother had stayed home to make breakfast for her was back when her brother and dad were around. She could feel her heartstrings begin to weep and a tear slithered down her cheek.

Her mom appeared behind her, grabbing her shoulders, and leaning over to kiss her on the forehead. She knew how hard today would be, so she was making sure she was there from the beginning; to try and make some of the day ok.

Her mom placed a plate of pancakes in front of Jane, smiling like a crazy person. If she'd tried to smile any harder, her eyes might have bulged out of her head.

They ate quietly, both secretly feeling humbled by each other. Jane still expected her mom to leave at any second. Pushing her chair back, Jane scooped up both empty plates, taking them to the sink and rinsing them before putting them into the dishwasher.

As she started to clean the rest of the mess her mom had made, her mom received a text message from their neighbor.

"Oh, it's Sandra…"

"What did she say?" Jane continued cleaning the benchtop.

"She's wondering whether you could walk with Theo to school today?"

"Theo? I thought he went to a private school?"

"Well apparently not anymore."

"Sure. I can do that."

"Thanks, Hun. I'll text her back." Her mom kissed her on the cheek and left Jane to finish the cleaning. She put her sneakers on, grabbed her keys and bag, then walked out the front door.

Theo was her childhood best friend. Five years before they had started high school, he had been diagnosed with autism. Jane couldn't imagine dealing with something like that. She never really saw his differences as a problem – he was her best friend and she loved him the way he was – but she knew sometimes life was more challenging for him, especially in social situations. Anyway, it wasn't easy starting a new school in general.

She and Theo used to have playdates when they were toddlers, their moms using it as an excuse to catch up. They used to hang out in the afternoons after elementary school too, but when they started going to different high schools that all changed. That was a long time ago now, Jane couldn't remember the last time she'd even said hello to him or his parents.

Their happy little moment this morning was short-lived. Jane almost burst into tears knowing that another morning like this probably wouldn't happen again until graduation, and that would only be if she was lucky.

Jane finished up the cleaning, checked all the windows and doors were locked, and grabbed her bag. Her phone beeped, showing a message from her mom.

Maybe she's sent me a sweet message, Jane thought.
LOVE YOU, HAVE A GREAT DAY SWEETIE.

Jane sighed and ran her hand through her long wavy hair. She went to reply but there was no point. She was pretty surprised that her mom even had time to message her. Maybe she was starting to make an effort again or something. Who knew?

Jane slipped her phone into her pocket, put on her jacket, and gave herself a final once over in the mirror by the front door. Jane was reminded of her dad when she looked at her reflection. She was taller than her mom, getting her height from her dad, and she had his emerald-green eyes. They were her favorite feature about herself. Everything else about her was just ordinary. Her lips weren't too thin but weren't too thick either. Her hair had a middle-of-the-road sandy color to it. She was slim but not skinny, curves where people wanted them but not too curvy. She would describe herself as an average-looking person.

She shrugged again, then swung her bag over her shoulder, grabbed her house keys and walked out the front door, locking it behind her. She made her way over to Theo's house.

*

Walking up the steps to Theo's front door, Jane could hear the commotion going on inside. She knocked lightly at first and then heavily. The door swung open revealing a very out of breath Sandra.

"Oh! Jane! Look at you; you've grown! You've caught me at a bad time, darling," she said.

Theo appeared in the hallway, cutting her off.

"Theo, it's Jane. She's going to walk with you to school today. She'll be able to tell you all about it, won't you, Jane?"

Theo stared at Jane for a moment, and then slowly smiled. It was the same goofy smile she remembered from back when they were kids. He was taller though, and he had more freckles scattered across his face. Must be from being outside all the time. His brown hair looked soft, and all of a sudden, she wanted to run her hands through it.

Her best friend, Poppy, would label him as "cute" and Jane was thinking the same. She nodded a yes towards Sandra and gave Theo a friendly smile back. She didn't know what to do with herself.

"Mrs-"

"Call me Sandra, dear."

"Uh ok, sorry, yeah, Sandra. I think I'll sit out here on the steps until Theo is ready, if that's all right with you?" She didn't want to stand on his toes.

"Sure, sure that would be great. Won't be long! C'mon Theo, hurry up. Go get your stuff so you won't be late for your first day."

Jane twisted around on her heels and sat down at the top of the steps. She looked out at the neighborhood, watching the buzz of kids begin their journey to their own schools. Waiting for Theo hadn't helped with her butterflies, and she swore they'd fly out of her ears any minute now.

The door finally opened behind her, and she stood up. Theo stepped outside, having finally got himself together.

Sandra let out a big huff of air, like she'd been holding it in all morning. She gave Theo a quick hug and a little shove in Jane's direction.

Jane headed down the steps, hoping Theo would follow. She moved to the side of the pavement, and Theo stepped up beside her. He was a head taller than her.

"So, are you excited?" she asked.

Theo looked down at his feet then back at Jane, shrugging in reply. His shyness seemed to suddenly overwhelm him. Hopefully it would ease once they arrived at school. If she was honest, she felt a little awkward hanging out with her childhood best friend again, but she had missed his presence.

*

Theo

Nerves rather than excitement filled Theo. He'd been going to the same school for years, and it had been familiar. The private school was strict, but Theo liked the routines. He liked knowing what was going to happen and when. It was predictable. It was safe.

He glanced down at Jane. He was a head taller than her and she… she was gorgeous.

It's not like Theo hadn't seen her before – they were childhood best friends – but something had changed since then. Her eyes were like a garden's new spring growth, bright and soft all at once. Curious too. Her hair was sandy and wavy, like it belonged to a surf beach. The way she smiled brought instant butterflies to him.

Theo was nervous around her, and not just because it was his first day at a new school. He had completely forgotten how to talk to his childhood best friend.

*

Jane

About twenty minutes later they stood across the road from Jane's school. The school had about a thousand students attending every year, sometimes more, sometimes less. It wasn't a small school but it was easy to feel like you knew everyone. Jane had one last year before they went out into the

13

big wide world and off to college. Jane's stomach churned at the thought.

Lost in her thoughts, Jane stepped out onto the road. She didn't notice the oncoming traffic; didn't see the car hurtling towards her. Theo grabbed her hand, tugging her backwards just in time.

Jane's heart hammered against her chest. She looked at their hands and then at him before giving a polite smile. "Thank you."

He let go, but his cheeks blossomed red.

Jane pretended not to notice. "Are you ready to go in?"

He gave a quick and sure nod and with that, they headed into the mayhem otherwise known as "high school".

The principal and a few other teachers hovered in the foyer inside. One of them greeted Jane with a warm smile. "New student?" she asked, gesturing towards Theo.

Jane nodded, but Theo gave no response. He looked around at the walls, his eyes darting from place to place.

It was the art teacher, evidenced by the paint on her hands and clothes. She reached out her hand to Theo to introduce herself. "Nice to meet you. I'm Mrs Green. Head on down to the gymnasium. Your grade is meeting there. They'll split you up into your homeroom classes." She gave Theo a bright smile and turned herself toward Jane. "Hi, Jane! Nice to see you again. How was your summer?"

"It was good, thank you. We better head toward the gymnasium. I'll see you later Mrs Green!" Jane said cheerily. She'd always loved Mrs Green.

Mrs Green gave them a small wave and then turned around to greet another student.

Jane already had a mental map of her high school, so she hurried off towards the gym. She noticed the familiar faces of the students in her grade, heading in the same direction. She gave a few small grimaces, but everyone seemed too busy to stop and talk. She hadn't seen any of her own friends yet. Maybe they'd be inside. Jane looked back at Theo,

hoping he was still following. Thankfully he was, but he looked a bit skittish.

In the gym, another teacher told them to take a seat wherever. Jane followed the other students like a sheep and sat a few feet away from everyone. Everyone seemed to have the same idea, and the class ended up quite spaced out. The only difference she noticed about the gym was that the bleachers were pushed to the side, making enough space for her whole year to take a seat on the ground. Jane still hadn't spotted any of her friends. She sent a message to her best friend, Poppy.

WHERE ARE YOU??? MY NEIGHBOR'S SON IS WITH ME. IT'S HIS FIRST DAY HERE.

Theo took a seat next to Jane and peered around. Jane swore she could almost feel his nerves rising through his skin. He swallowed hard and started to rock.

Jane took off her bag and got comfortable. She felt thankful for it being the last time she'd have to go through this. It was always a nerve-racking experience, especially when you're awkwardly waiting for at least one friend to turn up.

"Hey, how was your summer? Excited to be back huh?" she said to the people around her, trying to start up a conversation.

A couple of others mumbled polite replies, which Jane appreciated, but no one seemed talkative. Strangely, seeing they were also anxious helped settle her nerves; everyone seemed to be in the same boat.

Theo's rocking became aggressive.

"Are you..." Jane stopped herself. It's probably a self-soothing thing, she thought. It reminded her of when they were kids, he couldn't keep still.

She gazed around the room. A few other students stared in her direction, well in Theo's direction. The students in her grade were whispering to each other and had begun pointing. Their reactions caused a wave of embarrassment to crash over her. It was only his first day and he was already gaining so much attention for his differences. Jane felt awkward and a thought of distancing herself popped into her head. She tried to dismiss it but hoped Theo would stop, otherwise he'd ruin his own chances for making friends.

The urge to shuffle away was strong, but that wasn't fair. Theo was a good guy. All those years she spent with him as a child were some of her happiest moments. He had pulled her out of the way of an oncoming car just about half an hour ago. She couldn't leave him.

She touched his hand, patting it three times. She didn't know any other way to help, but she remembered that when they were little, Sandra would do this to calm him whenever he felt overwhelmed. She wasn't sure whether it would work, considering they weren't kids anymore; they were seventeen. She still hoped that sent an "I'm here" message to him.

Theo hesitated. For a moment, Jane thought she'd made things worse, then he resumed his rocking. It was just a slight back and forth movement now though, Jane's reassurance seemingly calming him.

The school bell went off.

The principal walked in with a few last students – finally, her friends! Always fashionably late.

Poppy's hair swished over her shoulder, hand entangled with her boyfriend, Nico's, as she scanned the crowd. She spotted Jane and pulled Nico over. Poppy was one of those people who could walk into a crowd and brighten everyone's lives with just a smile.

Poppy and Jane met in their sophomore year of high school. Jane had seen her around a lot during her freshman year but never had the confidence to walk up to her, until her second year where they were placed in the same photography class. Jane absolutely loved photography and she couldn't be more thrilled when she realized Poppy felt the same. They bonded over it, becoming closer than anyone else Jane was friends with at the time. That's how Jane ended up in the most popular group in the school. Poppy had introduced her into it, and it kind of just clicked.

Jack walked in after them with a few of his other friends. He made his way over to the rest of the group. He had a different haircut and his arms looked bigger as well. Jane already felt herself swooning over him again. Every year, her crush came back when school restarted. She'd never thought about acting upon it because he never showed that he liked her back in that way. Maybe he was using the rule of treat them mean to keep them keen.

"Hello, everyone. How was your summer?" the principal began.

No one answered of course. Jane glanced around at the people on either side of her. They looked just as confused by the question as she was.

"I know you must all be very nervous," he continued, "but this is just another first day, only this time for your last year of high school."

Poppy and Nico finally sat down next to Jane. Poppy gave her a small hug and nodded her head toward Theo.

"Is this the guy you messaged me about earlier? Your neighbor?" Poppy whispered.

"Yeah, he's a bit nervous."

"Must be hard going to a new school in your final year, so that's expected." Shrugging, she trained her attention toward the principal.

"Hey, man, I'm Nico." Nico held out a hand to Theo.

Theo nodded and mumbled his name in reply. He shook Nico's hand timidly.

The principal started to list the school rules as per usual, such as no phones out during class without special permission, or if it's an emergency. He then explained how the classes would work this year. To start with, Jane and the other students would head to their "homeroom" classes and then disperse into different classes every period; again, as per usual. Jane didn't know why he felt like he had to explain this, but she guessed it didn't hurt. It would be useful for Theo at least.

Jane found herself zoning out. She tuned back in when the vice-principal took to the stage. He began calling names and directing students to different teachers.

Jane felt panic rising in her. She hoped she was in homeroom class with some of her friends. She glanced at Theo. If she felt this nervous about it all, even though she'd been through it three times before, how must he be feeling? She didn't know how he would handle this. She probably should've explained more about how her school worked this morning, considering she knew nothing about how his old school was organized.

"We'll probably be split up. I'm not sure if your old school did the same," she told him quickly. "But I'll meet you outside the school gates at the end of the day."

He didn't answer, so all Jane could do was hope he absorbed the information.

"Can I have your phone for a sec?" Jane asked.

Theo slowly handed it over to her. Jane scrolled through his contacts and added herself in. "You can text me if you need me," she said, handing the phone back. She wasn't sure if he would, but at least it eased her conscience a little at having to leave him.

Theo stared at the phone for a moment, then put it back in his pocket.

Half the students had gone by then, their names already called. Surely, it would be their turn soon, Jane thought. And of course, as soon as she thought that, Theo's name was called.

He didn't move.

"Theodore Williams?" the teacher called again.

Jane gave him a little shove to get him going but stopped when he went pale.

"It'll be ok," she whispered. She tried to give him a convincing smile along with a big thumbs up.

He stood slowly, and made his way through the crowd, steering himself around students before joining his class group. She saw Jack give him a nasty stare before hopping

up as his name was also called. Jane's thoughts about her crush returning halted. She had never seen that expression on Jack's face before.

Jack casually made his way toward the same homeroom teacher as Theo's and walked just behind him. Jack was hot, funny, and an all-rounder, but he still could be a dick. If Jane was being honest, she wasn't quite sure why she had feelings towards him. All of a sudden, when she thought about Jack giving Theo a hard time, any attraction she felt towards him completely disappeared.

The teacher cleared his throat, clearly annoyed at the delay, then began leading the group out of the gym.

Theo looked back at Jane one last time before following the rest of his classmates. Jane couldn't help thinking he looked so innocent, she could've just about gone and cuddled him. And then he was gone, disappearing from sight as the teacher led him away.

She returned her attention to the vice-principal, and her butterflies flared up once again.

3.

Jane

Jane got into a routine of going over to Theo's house in the mornings and walking to school with him. Sometimes, if their classes were close together, she'd walk Theo to his class before going on to her own. Whenever she did, she could feel the stares of her classmates. It was worse for Theo though. She'd heard his name being tossed around the school. Or rather, the nickname they'd given him. They called him "The Freak", which made her stomach turn. The name was Jack's creation. Jane's crush was completely gone, her dislike for Jack increasing ever since then.

It started on the first day. The bell had just gone off for their lunch break, and Jane had walked out of English with Theo. The class hadn't changed very much, except for a couple of new posters and a different table arrangement. It still had an old and dreary look but most of the classrooms were the same. She'd been explaining to him about how lunch worked at her school, but Theo hadn't seemed that interested. Instead, he'd wanted to tell her about butterflies.

In the English class, the teacher had made them do an activity to get them thinking creatively. They had to do a small paragraph using "Zoomorphism" – which was when something was described like an animal.

"I wanted to do a butterfly, but I couldn't choose which type. I thought about Red Admirals or Monarchs, because I see them most often, but my favorite is the Tierra del Fuego butterfly. They're from Brazil, you know."

Jane never knew there were so many butterflies, but the more Theo talked the more she remembered his interest in being in the garden when they were kids. She got stuck in the memory when someone's arm slid across her shoulders.

"Tear de fuggly what?" Jack stared at Theo, and Jane could tell he hadn't really misheard, he was just making fun of Theo.

20

"Tierra del Fuego butterfly," Theo repeated quietly. He didn't meet Jack's eye.

Jack stared at Theo for a moment longer and then turned to Jane. "Hey, Jane, you coming or what? Oh, I'm Jack by the way." He put his hand out to shake.

Theo raised his hand to take Jack's, but Jack cheekily took it away. Theo's face dropped, his excitement diminished. Jane already missed it.

"Were you guys really talking about butterflies?" Jack asked.

"Yeah, don't you remember what we learned about in English?" Jane said while trying to move from under his arm. She felt his hand grip her shoulder. Was he trying to assert his dominance over her to show Theo who's boss or something?

"And you chose to do it about butterflies?" Jack pointed his question toward Theo.

"Yeah, they're cool." Theo said, not adding any detail like he did before with Jane.

"That's kind of a freak thing to talk about. Butterflies of all things, dude?"

"Jack, don't be mean." Jane found the urge to back Theo up. Jack's grip tightened on her shoulder. This wasn't the Jack she had crushed on. How had she never noticed this?

"I'm not, I'm just saying. Anyway, we're going to lunch. See you around, Freak." He covered his hand with his mouth, making an "oops" sound. "I mean Theo, my bad." He turned Jane around, walking her down the hallway.

Jane had looked back over her shoulder. Theo watched them walk away, disgust written all over his face.

Even now, the memory made Jane's stomach feel hollow. It wasn't his fault he was the way he was. It wasn't his choice, but most of her classmates were still too immature to realize this.

Jane had also heard her name tossed around, adopting an unwelcome nickname too. It only passed around in her friend group – it was just a little tease they would tell her. They called her "The Freak's Friend". She tried to ignore it for Theo's sake. But after what had happened, she had started to distance herself from Theo. She didn't really notice she was doing it at first. She had shown him where all his classes were the first few days but now only walks with him to and from school. She hadn't really seen him much at school anyway, just in a class or two and sometimes at lunch in the art room.

She had to admit, the nickname had made it harder for him to make friends. No one was really giving him a chance after what happened with Jack. She was still pissed at Jack, but all her friends still hung out with him, so she couldn't say much.

Jane was determined to carry on with her life, not even bothering to acknowledge the name calling. Thankfully, she and Poppy were in the same homeroom class which made everything easier. Poppy was also in two of her other classes – geography, which Nico was in too, and photography. Her homeroom teacher had tried to make her class inviting, so there was an old couch at the back and a few bean bags scattered around. Since Poppy and Jane were one of the first ones in, they decided to take a seat on the couch.

"Hey, Poppy, Theo isn't that bad right?" she asked Poppy in homeroom one day. "Have you heard what they've been calling him?"

"Yeah…" Poppy's long brown hair was slicked into a high ponytail, and she ran her fingers through it. She had a set of new acrylics on, and Jane wondered how they didn't get caught.

Jane felt something in the air shift. She could tell Poppy didn't want to make her feel bad, but it was obvious Poppy didn't want her to be talking about Theo. It was a horrible feeling. Jane felt herself wobble.

Poppy caught her eye, and then she quickly looked down. Her face turned stern as she avoided looking at Jane. Her lips drew into a straight line which was a rare occurrence. Poppy never acted like this. Ever since they first became friends, she had never even seen Poppy behave in this way. Jane and Nico were probably the only ones who knew Poppy was a secret

over-thinker. Was she ashamed that she was best friends with "The Freak's Friend"? Was the group getting to her that much?

Even though Poppy was one of those people who could light up a room, she could also darken it. Jane would normally call her one of her best friends, but right now it felt the opposite. Maybe Poppy was more worried about her image than Jane was.

Jane didn't want to make someone else feel the same way she did. And that made her feel really ashamed. She remembered back to when she and Theo used to play as children, and she never thought anything of his disability. Now it was constantly on her mind.

"Um, I just wanted to ask you about…" Jane scrambled for an excuse, "the project after lunch, in geography?"

Poppy mumbled her way through an explanation of the project, all of which Jane already knew, of course. As soon as she could, Jane stood up, asked for a hallway pass, and walked away.

She ended up walking to the bathroom, putting the toilet lid down and sitting there until the bell went off. Maybe she shouldn't have avoided Theo after all. He would have happily talked to her, wouldn't he?

*

The next day, Jane avoided the courtyard, this was because she didn't feel like seeing  anyone she knew. She decided to go find a tree to sit under while she ate her lunch. The tree she found seemed like a nice spot and she sat down. She had no idea how big of a mistake she was making. Out of the corner of her eye, she saw an object hurtling towards her, but it was already too late to move. A football hit her smack on the shoulder.

Pretty perfectly aimed, Jane thought. She'd dropped the sandwich she was eating, and it was already too late to recover it.

Jack ran up to her, his blonde hair bouncing, his muscles working to retrieve the ball. "Sorry about that, Duke has some really bad aim."

So he says, Jane thought, but she had trouble believing the hit was unintentional. Maybe he mistook the word "bad" for "perfect".

He was so tall that his shadow fell over her. He held out his hand to help her get up.

"What are you doing over here?"

Jane didn't feel like explaining herself, so she just shrugged in reply.

"You do know you're sitting on the field, don't you? Where balls fly around?"

"Yes. I do know," Jane said, her cheeks flushing. "It can also be a place where you can sit," she said defensively.

"Well… if that's the case, watch out for balls coming your way." Jack turned away. He was proving to be even more of a dick than she realized. Jane heard him mutter something under his breath about how The Freak must have been getting to her.

Jane knew after that incident if she wanted to sit alone she would have to find another spot, otherwise she would become target practice.

That day, Jane really looked forward to her time walking home with Theo. She could see him coming more and more out of his shell – becoming the Theo she used to know when they were kids.

She could tell he knew she distanced herself from him during the school day, but again he didn't seem to mind.

"What happened in the land of Theo today?"

"I painted butterflies in art class. Monarchs, a Small Copper, and a Common Blue. Did you know the Common Blue isn't very common in America… because it's a European butterfly." Theo laughed to himself at his own joke before telling her more facts about the Common Blue.

Jane knew he must love butterflies because it was becoming a theme in their conversations. She liked how he

was so interested in them, but mostly she just liked his voice which drowned out her own thoughts.

*

Finally, it was Friday, the last day of their first week. Jane waited at the gates for Theo, but Jack came along instead. He put his arm over her shoulders. Jack had done this a few times over the years, and it used to make her heart race, but after what had happened earlier in the week it felt different. It revolted her.

"Hey, Jane! Freak's Friend, why do you even hang out with The Freak anyway?" he quizzed her.

Jane thought about not answering and just shrugging him off, but she had a feeling it would just make his pestering worse. "He's not a freak and my mom asked me to. We've been friends since we were little."

"Ohhh… so you never wanted to in the first place, huh? That's a shame. Could always ditch him, ya know?" He completely disregarded the fact they were friends when they were little. He didn't know how badly Jane wanted to though, right in that moment. She hated the nicknames Jack came up with for her and Theo. She did not want to be called "The Freak's Friend" even if Jack was only teasing.

"Yeah, well, I'm just helping him out for a while. Imagine if you had to come into a school where everyone already had their friend groups set up and everything," she said.

"Whatever. See ya around, Freak's Friend." Jack took his arm off Jane's shoulders, winked at her, and followed his friends toward the parking lot.

Jane hadn't managed to find the time or motivation to go and get her license over summer but obviously most of her friend group had. Actually, most of her grade had. Jane watched as they hopped into Jack's car. His daddy must have bought it for him since it was a BMW and she was pretty sure Jack didn't have a job. She was frozen in her tracks. Jack's eyes followed her, and she couldn't take her eyes off him

25

either. He started to do a burn out before racing out of the parking lot entrance, right next to where she was standing, a cheeky smirk on his face. This repulsed Jane even more.

Sam and Tommy's laughter reached her from the car, and Brittany squealed as they went into a little drift before they straightened up and drove away.

Jane cursed herself for not sticking up for herself or for Theo, but it was too late now. She kicked at the ground and let out a frustrated sigh. If Theo had just shown up when he was supposed to, she wouldn't have had to talk to Jack who was now convincing her that he was a dick the whole time she'd known him. It was crazy how fast feelings can change once you begin to see someone's true colors.

"Jane?"

Jane whipped around. Theo stood right behind her. Heat rose in her cheeks. How long had he been standing there?

"Hey, Theo," she said, lightly trying to cover her embarrassment. "Let's get going. I have to make my mom and I dinner tonight." Jane burst into a fast-paced walk. Theo jogged to catch up to her. She could feel an awkward silence in the air. She swallowed, realizing she would have to address it.

"You heard what Jack and I said, didn't you? I'm sorry. I don't know what his problem is."

Theo just shrugged in return and looked down at his feet. "They shouldn't call you The Freak. Everyone is too quick to judge. Don't worry about it. I'm sure it won't last long, once they get to know you."

Theo shook his head. "It only just registered with me that the nickname I've been hearing all week is actually my nickname," he said.

"Oh… I thought you knew. I'm sorry, Theo." Guilt raged through Jane. Theo increased their pace.

"My whole life I've been an outcast. At my old school it wasn't much different except the teachers helped me out a lot more, and I actually had a few friends who were like me. But I'm not even that different, y'know?"

"I know and I'm sorry and—"

"No, you don't know, Jane. You don't know. I've adopted a nickname in my first week, on the first day! That must be a world record. I don't know why I thought this school would be different. Maybe because I knew you would be here, and we were friends when we were kids. I thought maybe we could be again…"

Jane didn't know what to say. Her heart wrenched for him, but she couldn't make it better.

Jane looked at him. His eyes couldn't seem to focus on one thing. She went to lift her hand onto his shoulder to give a little reassurance, but before she could do that he ran off.

"Theo, wait!" Jane called, but she guessed nothing would stop him. She sighed. It was going to be a long year.

4.

Jane

It was only a couple of weeks until the break, and the weather was getting cooler. As the school year had progressed, Jane had continued to walk to and from school with Theo, every day. She was really starting to warm up to him.

Everything about him started to interest her. She still hung out with the popular group, and Theo was finally making some of his own acquaintances, though he mostly stuck by himself.

Whenever Jane saw Jack around school, it was never in a group setting. He seemed to purposely seek her out when she was alone. He would always lean in uncomfortably close and whisper, "Just for a while, huh?" before snickering and strolling away.

The friend groups that had formed throughout her freshman year at school had mostly stayed the same over the years. Jack was in the popular group, the clique everyone strived to be in. Poppy was also in that group. Jane could tell she wasn't exactly proud of being in the group now. Jack wasn't the only one who could be a dick, and a lot of their humor leaned towards unkindness. But Poppy wasn't willing to leave the group either.

Outside of them, there was the sporty group – though most of those girls were a part of the popular group too – then there were the artsy kids, the nerds, and of course the loners… though that was basically just Theo.

Not everyone fit into a classified group though – some students didn't belong to one or had friends in more than one group. Jane sometimes wished she was one of the students who didn't belong to any group. It seemed easier than constantly having to live up to other people's expectations or deal with people like Jack.

Jane struggled at times, and thought about giving everything up then and there, but she couldn't do that to her

mom. She felt a little guilt towards Theo too. She thought that maybe Theo's nickname would've been dropped after a few weeks. Clearly, that had been wishful thinking. She still couldn't leave him by himself to walk to and from school even though she knew he would be fine. Her mom would have been disappointed in her if she stopped helping out. She'd say something along the lines of having raised Jane better than that. Deep in thought, Jane felt someone nudge her, bringing her back to reality. Theo looked at her, a concerned expression across his face. Jane snapped out of it instantly. Man, how long had she been swimming in her thoughts? She glanced around. They were only a few streets from their homes. She didn't even remember walking out of the school gates, it was as if she was on autopilot.

"Jane, where'd you go?" he asked.

"Oh, you know, I went to space."

"Physically, you can't go to space, unless you have trained for eight years, then been chosen for a mission."

"I know, I know Theo I'm just pulling your leg—"

"No, you're not. You're not touching me."

"It's a figure of speech, Theo." It always fascinated Jane how Theo could understand similes, but metaphors often confused him. Just that one extra step of abstraction was too much. "I'm just teasing you. Anyway, I can always go to mental space," Jane said. She looked at Theo, and imagined his brain cranking its gears, trying to figure out what she meant, "You know, when you just stare at one spot and things go a little blurry; like zoning out and you kind of go-to 'space'." She made air quotes around the word "space", hoping he would grasp her meaning.

"I never thought about going to 'mental space'." He added his own air quotes.

Jane laughed and raised her hand to ruffle his hair. He instantly hit her hand away and smoothed his hair back into place. This just made Jane laugh harder. Theo stared at her, confusion lining his face.

Jane tried to calm down, but new giggles burst from her every time she looked at him.

"Why are you laughing?"

"I don't know, Theo. You're just so serious sometimes, and it makes me laugh."

Theo shrugged in response. Jane's laughter petered out. They turned the corner, and Jane saw their two houses down at the end of the street. She could almost imagine they had spread their arms out ready to welcome them home.

"Anyway, it's ok to be serious. It's not a bad thing. You know that don't you, Theo?" Jane paused, waiting for his reply, "Theo?"

"Yeah, yeah, I know. It's just the other kids at school laugh at me for the same reason. It's only ok for you to laugh at me about it," he replied.

Jane felt a rush of protective anger go through her veins.

"Yeah well, those kids don't know what they are missing out on," she said firmly. "And they're only laughing because they don't understand." She knew it probably wouldn't make him feel any better, but it was true.

She snuck a look at him. She was a little gobsmacked that he had just told her that it was ok for her to laugh at him. She was never sure how he felt about her, other than being the girl who walked with him to and from school, but perhaps he was really starting to see her as a friend again. Maybe he always had.

Just before they split off in different directions to their own front doors, Jane patted his hand three times. He didn't respond, his fingers remaining clutched around his bag strap, but something about patting his hand made Jane feel calm. It seemed to have the same effect for him too.

He looked down at her hand touching his, and before he had a chance to look back up, Jane ruffled his hair again and sprinted away to her porch steps.

She unlocked the door, then looked back at Theo. He stood where she'd left him, trying to get his hair back in place.

She threw him a mischievous grin. "I'll see you tomorrow!"

5.

Jane

Halfway through October, Jane's school was trying a new school break system. It was called their pre-winter break. They'd just had nine weeks and four days of school and today was their last day before they had a week off.

Apparently, they were considering doing this every year as it was supposed to help with the students' mental state. After the week off, they then would have to wait until their winter break for another vacation.

Jane and Poppy couldn't be more thrilled about the time off. Poppy couldn't stop talking about it. She'd started to make plans, which included a group trip to the beach in the middle of fall. Jane thought Poppy was crazy, but she would be keen to go just to get out of the house.

On the last day before their pre-winter break Jane felt happy. It wasn't because she didn't normally like her subjects or the work. It was still the same problem. No one had made any effort to warm up to Theo, and she was still being teased in her group about being the freak's friend. Maybe if she hung out with her group over this week, or simply with Poppy and Nico, then they would ease off a bit.

Her last day of school dragged on as every class she had piled her with homework, but Jane couldn't have felt more at peace.

*

Jane spent the first day of the pre-winter break sunbathing in her backyard. Or trying to, at least. It was about 2 p.m., and the sun was barely out. It was spending the day behind the clouds. Even though she was "sunbathing" fully clothed and had her forest green puffer coat on, she was still happy, and she had no worries. All her concerns dropped away when school stopped. She felt like she rediscovered herself when

she was away from school. Even though the breaks could get pretty lonely, she still enjoyed them. No one to tease her, no one to avoid, and no one could call her names in her own backyard.

This particular afternoon, she heard someone moving around next to her. Well not right next to her. In the backyard next to hers; Theo's backyard. She could see him kneeling, inspecting some plants, being so careful not to harm them in any way. She thought it was quite sweet how much interest he paid them. She found herself smiling, feeling even more at peace. She leaned back into her chair, closing her eyes, and fell into a cosy slumber.

"Jane? Jane, are you ok? Do I have to come over? Jane, can you hear me?"

Jane woke, hearing a mumble of a voice. She shivered, the air suddenly cool against her skin. Gosh, the sun must've gone behind a cloud, she thought. It had been. All day.

"Janeeeeeeee!"

Who is that? Jane creaked her eyes open and was surprised to see the sky had deepened to a dark blue. She estimated it was probably only about 15 minutes to pitch black. How long had she been asleep for?

"Jane! Jane, Jane, Jane, Jane, Janeee!" yelled a voice from over the fence.

She snapped her head in the direction of the yelling and squinted her eyes. Theo.

"Theo, Theo, Theo, Theo!" she replied with a shout. "Sorry, I was sleeping. Thanks for waking me, I guess."

"Why were you sleeping outside? Normally people sleep in beds."

"It was just, so peaceful. I didn't mean to sleep for this long."

"Maybe set an alarm next time."

"Yeah, good idea."

Jane could see him twiddling his fingers and looking at the ground. She wondered what was on his mind, but before she could ask, he started telling her anyway.

"It's just that I saw you fall asleep when I was outside earlier this afternoon. You hardly moved all day, and then you weren't waking up."

"Were you worried about me, Theodore Williams?" Jane threw him a cheeky smile. Hopefully, he could tell she was having fun with him.

"Well, yeah I was, Janie. It's just tha—"

"Whoa, whoa, whoa," Jane interrupted him. "Did you just call me Janie?"

"I couldn't think of anything else to make your name longer. Because you called me Theodore, so I just thought I could call you Janie."

Somehow, this just made Jane smile more. "Alright, alright Theodore. Good point. Sorry for interrupting. What were you saying?"

He looked down towards his hands again. There was a big pause before he spoke again. Jane waited patiently, not wanting him to feel pressured.

"It's just that I kept looking out the window, expecting you to have woken up but you didn't. And you looked so cold. You started to physically shake and yes, Janie…" He paused and looked at Jane, a smirk crossing his face. "I was worried about you."

He was worried… that was new. Sweet though, Jane thought to herself.

"Sorry to make you worry, Theo. No one should be worrying on the pre-winter break. I'll make sure to set an alarm next time, just in case."

"Ok, please do, or I'll have to wake you up again. Goodnight, Janie."

And with that abrupt ending, he walked inside. Jane thought she was finally getting through to him, but suddenly, he just completely closed himself off again. He must have felt too awkward.

Jane sighed and pulled herself up out of the old sun lounger. It creaked under her weight as she got off it. Her legs were stiff from sitting too long. She shook them out and turned

toward the house. Before she made it to her back door, she whispered a quiet goodnight and a thank-you in Theo's direction.

To Jane's surprise, her mom walked through the front door just as she got inside. Crap! Jane thought she had more time to make dinner. Her mom would be expecting it to be ready for her right now. She looked up, and confusion crossed her face.

"Why are you coming through the back door?" she asked.

"Why are you coming through the front door?" Jane hit back. She sprinted to the kitchen, throwing a pot of water on the stove. Pasta in sauce with cheese on top – that would make a quick, easy dinner.

Jane's mom followed her into the kitchen, then just shrugged. Jane could tell she couldn't be bothered questioning Jane any further. Must have been a hard day at work. Jane could always see the exhaustion on her mother's face, just by how drawn her face was and how dark under her eyes were. Her hair was also a mess. Perhaps it required too much energy to put it back into place. She'd probably given all her energy to someone else at the hospital, and she had nothing left. Maybe one of her patients had died. Jane felt morbid thinking that, but it was probably true.

"Dinner will be ready in around twenty minutes," Jane told her.

Her mom just nodded and headed upstairs. To have a shower and wash off work, Jane guessed.

*

Around twenty minutes later, Jane's mom came back downstairs and sat down at the table. Jane grabbed two bowls and served up the pasta. She picked her mom's favorite bowls, the white ones with the blue line around the rim. One of them had a crack running down the middle of it, and she hoped it wasn't going to fall apart in her hands.

35

She grated some parmesan on top and carried the bowls over to the table. All was quiet, and an awkward heaviness sat between them.

"Everything alright?" Jane asked, between forkfuls of pasta.

"Oh… you know, darling. Same old, same old."

"Same old… as in someone dying today?"

Jane had tried to get her mom to open up a bit more lately. Ever since Jane's dad passed away; he died while serving in the army, before she started high school – her mom had been keeping everything to herself. She wasn't coping well with the occasional deaths at the hospital.

Jane knew it must be incredibly hard to be a nurse. Her mom had a lot to learn about her patients, trying to connect with them instantly, to make them feel comfortable, and then they got discharged or worse, passed away. Sometimes her mom had to be there for them when they died. Jane couldn't imagine how she did it.

"Don't be so blunt, Jane." Her mom paused, swallowing. "But yes, someone did pass away. I've been his nurse for about two months. We always knew how it would end, but everyone had so much hope. He passed probably thirty minutes before my shift ended, so at least I was there for him." Tears started to stream down her face.

Jane stood, pushing the chair away with her knees. She slipped into the lounge and grabbed a box of tissues and a picture of her dad. Inside the frame, he held her mom, both of them with hope-filled eyes. They were so in love.

She walked back over to her mom, passing her the tissues and then the picture frame. Sometimes it made her feel better when she could physically hug him when she needed him. Jane sat down on the ground at her mom's feet. She put her head on her mother's lap and danced her fingers along her shin. They stayed like that for a good ten minutes, letting their dinner go cold.

Jane's mom let out a big sigh and had a little laugh to herself. "Gosh, I needed that. It's good to have a cry."

Jane knew this was her trying to reason with herself, about letting everything out. She wanted everything to be ok.

"Come here and give your mom a hug."

Jane stood and so did her mom. Jane gave her the biggest hug she could manage. She felt her mother relax into her, the hug helping.

Her mom broke the embrace by pushing Jane out at arm's length and giving her a once over, before bringing her back in and kissing her on the forehead. "I need to sleep baby. I've got a shift early in the morning."

With that, she let go of Jane and made her way upstairs and into bed.

Jane rolled her shoulders, trying to let out the tension she was holding. She turned around to see their barely eaten dinners. She took a few more bites of hers, and then put the rest in Tupperware for her mom to take for lunch the next day. She rinsed the bowls, placing them on the benchtop.

Grabbing her phone, Jane locked all the doors and closed all the windows, before turning off the lights and heading upstairs to bed.

6.

Jane

The next day, Jane woke at around 8 a.m. She'd never been the type of person to sleep in, even during vacation, so she swung her legs out of bed and headed to the bathroom.

After showering, she wrapped herself in a towel and sat on the edge of her bed. She scrolled through her phone, going through her social media. Poppy had just posted on Instagram. It was a photo of her and Nico, cuddling at the local beach.

Jane tapped on the comment section. She typed out a comment saying "YOU TWO ARE MAD! IT'S ALMOST WINTER, CUTE THO!!" and tapped confirm. She was the eighth person to comment. It remined her that Poppy had a lot of friends and made her thankful that Jane was one of her closest.

She sighed, dropping the phone on the bed beside her. She looked around at her room. Her dad's old record player sat in the corner, underneath it, a bookshelf bursting with books. Photos covered half her walls. She adored photography and at any chance she got she always tried to improve. Most of the photos were of her town's landscape, and a few of her friends and family. Her favorites were the ones she had taken with her disposable camera. Just the texture, lighting, and not knowing how it would turn out until it was developed excited her. If she didn't feel like hanging with anyone on her free periods or at lunch, she would usually be in the photography class developing photos or working on her project.

Other than that, her room just had her everyday functional things.

She lost herself in a trance but shook herself out of it. She got up to look in her closet. It was a nice, crisp, fall day, so she chose one of her favorite dresses – a ditsy daisy, tie at the shoulder dress. It was really a summer dress but with a

long-sleeve turtleneck underneath she could wear it for fall too.

She was surprised by how much better it made her feel. Brushing her hair, she let it flow down over her shoulders. She'd always loved her hair. In different lights it changed color, but usually it had a sandy appearance. She only wore it down at home, so she truly felt herself today.

She grabbed a book on her way downstairs. It was one of her favorites – The Book Thief by Markus Zusak. She loved everything about it. It was one of those books she could read a million times and still react emotionally as if she was reading it for the first time. She intended to read it outside so she swung her coat over her shoulder, but she paused when she saw the dishes lying out from the night before. She sighed. She really should make a start on those first.

Jane went to turn on the faucet. A note lay beside the sink.

*Jane*

*Thanks for always being there for me. You're a real sweetheart. Sorry I can never hang out. Tomorrow morning (because I'm doing a double tonight) we should set a date in the calendar for just you and me to hang out. Maybe a girl's shopping trip? Love you so much,*

*Mom xx*

She folded the note up and held it up to her heart. Despite herself, a single tear slipped down her cheek. It had been years since her mom had left a note. Every one she got, she made sure to treasure. She placed it inside her book, keeping it safe.

After finishing the dishes, she made herself some toast and a milkshake, enjoying the indulgence of it. Smoothies were overrated. She brought her breakfast outside, placing it down next to her lounger.

The birds sang proudly, and a brisk wind shifted the leaves on the trees into swirling patterns. The sun would soon be peeking out over the top of the house, and then it would be a perfect day.

She smiled to herself. She grabbed her book and began reading while eating her breakfast.

Jane spent the whole morning there, only leaving her chair a few times, mostly to go to the bathroom or to get refreshments; sometimes snacks. At one point, she had to sprint through the house to receive the daily mail and to say a quick hello to the local mailman, Gary.

Just after lunch, she received a text message. Jane almost jumped out of her skin from the sound of it. Who on earth could be messaging her?

Putting her book down on her lap, she picked up her phone. She turned it over. *One new message from Poppy...*

Jane giggled with excitement and swiped it open. To Jane's surprise, it was a selfie of Poppy at the beach with the message: JOIN US TOMORROW?

Jane's giggles increased for a moment. She couldn't believe it. Poppy had actually invited her to the beach in the middle of fall!

Jane's thumbs flew, as she typed out a reply, then she stopped herself.

She should play it cool, or shouldn't she?

Ugh. Her over-anxious brain drove her nuts. Jane started to wish Poppy had never messaged in the first place.

No. That was a lie. And why would Poppy care anyway? They messaged all the time, so Jane wasn't sure where her anxious spell was coming from.

She should ask her mom first, but then again, why did it matter? Her mom was hardly ever home anyway.

Jane opened the message again and typed a simple "SURE" and pressed send.

Jane frowned at the phone. Maybe that was too cool. Maybe Poppy would think she wasn't interested at all. What if she changed her mind and took the invitation back?

Jane smooshed a pillow into her face and groaned against it. Seriously, what was wrong with her? Her phone beeped, another message coming through.

AWESOME! BRING YOUR SWIMSUIT. WILL YOU MEET US THERE OR DO YOU NEED A RIDE?

Jane hadn't thought about how she would get there. She'd have to ask her mom, unless she could just walk. Maybe it was too far away, but if she left early enough, she could meet them there.

Jane looked at the message again. Poppy *did* ask if she wanted a ride. Jane may as well take her up on it.

SORRY, MY MOM IS WORKING SO CAN'T DROP ME OFF. COULD YOU PICK ME UP PLEASE? TOTALLY OK IF YOU CAN'T THO!

Jane put her phone down. Her knees bounced, nerves working their way through her. Butterflies boiled in her stomach, as her head filled with endless questions. What was she going to wear? Did she even own a swimsuit?

Her phone dinged one more time, cutting off her spiraling thoughts.

SWEET! I'LL PICK YOU UP AT 10. I'LL DRIVE US.

Jane's butterflies settled down to a simmer, she hadn't had an episode of anxiety in ages.

She let out a breath and unclenched her hands, stretching out her fingers. She sent a quick message saying she couldn't wait, and then put her phone back down.

Nerves prickled up her arms. She rubbed her skin, thinking she'd just turn her nerves into excitement. A smile spread across her face, and she felt like dancing but resisted the urge. Instead, she sat back down in the lounger and lifted her book to start reading again, this time with the biggest grin spread across her face.

*

Jane could hardly sleep that night; she couldn't stop thinking. She had gone through all her clothes and swimsuits, but nothing seemed good enough. She wasn't even sure whether they would be going swimming since the temperature of the water would be below freezing. She didn't know why she was so worried about it. She had hung with her group outside of school before. She ended up falling asleep with her mess all around her.

At 8 a.m., she woke to her alarm blaring. She reached over to shut it up. Her hand fumbled and knocked one of her photo frames over. It fell and the glass smashed all over the ground. Now she felt awake. Bolting straight upright, she found the alarm and shut it off, then inspected the mess. Yawning, she reached down to pick up the broken frame. The photo of her with her brother and dad peered up at her; one of her favorites. She pressed her finger to her mouth, kissing it and then touching her brother and dad's face in the photo. She hadn't seen her brother in forever. Jane didn't even know whether he was alive.

She shook the remaining glass from the frame into the bin, then propped the photo back up on her bedside table. She stood, carefully avoiding the broken shards, then looked around the room. She couldn't quite face cleaning it up, so she walked out of her room and into her mother's.

Her mom was about the same size as her and had surprisingly good taste for a mom. Surely she wouldn't mind if Jane borrowed a swimsuit? Jane went through her mom's wardrobe until she found a nice, black one-piece.

It fit Jane perfectly, except it had quite a low back. Jane wasn't sure about showing that much skin. She almost took it off, but then she hesitated, looking at herself in the mirror. Maybe it would be ok? Afterall, she didn't exactly have another suit to choose from. She shrugged at her reflection.

Jane headed to the bathroom to finish getting ready, putting on some deodorant and sunscreen, then brushing her teeth and heading back to her room. The broken glass and piles of clothes greeted her. Jane did her best to clean up the shards, wrapping them in newspaper before throwing them in the bin. Then she turned to the clothes. Going through them, she

started to sort her mess out. All she needed was a good pair of Levi's jeans but, of course, they would be at the bottom of one of her many piles. Finally, she settled on some baggy white Levi's that she folded up at the bottom. She added a thermal, which she tucked into the front of her jeans, then threw on a hoodie. The hoodie was also one of her favorites. It had a patchwork effect to it which she loved.

It was nearly 9 a.m. She had an hour until Poppy would be there. She brushed out her hair and put on her dad's old baseball cap, then grabbed a tote bag and threw in all the beach necessities. She dropped her stuff by her door and turned back to the task of tidying her room.

Jane was just finishing up, when a ding sounded from the other side of her room. She rushed to her phone, noticing the time. It was nearly ten a.m.

She opened Poppy's message.  WILL BE THERE IN 5!

Jane grabbed her bag and sprinted down the stairs, taking them two at a time. She'd been so absorbed in cleaning her room, she had forgotten about the time. Rushing around, she checked everything was locked and found an old pair of sneakers which she didn't mind getting sandy. She filled up her water bottle and threw a bag of chips in her bag.

Through the kitchen window, she saw Poppy and Nico pull up to the house.

The phone in her hand dinged again, it was Poppy saying she was outside.

Jane ran towards the front door, slipping on the mat on the way there. She opened the door awkwardly, trying to jiggle her keys out of her bag. Poppy smiled from the car, and Jane gave her a quick wave. She locked the door and ran down the porch steps.

"Hey, girl!" Poppy jumped out of her car and opened the door for Jane.

"Hey…" Jane smiled sheepishly at Poppy.

Poppy gestured for her to get in, then jumped back in behind the driver's wheel.

Nico swiveled round in his seat, so he was half facing Jane and half facing Poppy.

"Hey, Jane."

"Hey, Nico. How are you?"

"Yeah, I'm pretty good, just been training for the track team really... did you know Theo joined? He's pretty damn good too!"

"Did he?" Jane almost yelled at Nico, making Poppy jump. "That's so cool! Yeah, he always goes for runs in the afternoon."

Poppy glanced back over her shoulder. "Geez, girl you gave me a fright!"

Jane blushed. "Sorry... I just got excited that's all."

"Theo's a pretty cool dude. I'm glad he's on the team," finished Nico.

There was a moment of silence where no one talked, and all they could hear was the road noise. Jane wished the radio was on, but Poppy caught her eye in the rearview mirror before she could ask.

"Cute outfit, girl!"

"Thanks! Who's meeting us at the beach? The usual? Also, I still can't believe we are going to the beach in like fifty-degree weather."

"Oh, you know... Jack... Nico, of course. Also, Sarah, Brittany, Julie, Michael, Sam, Tommy, and Lucas." Poppy rattled off the names.

Jane was surprised that most of the group was going to make it.

"Oh, actually not Brittany," Poppy added. "She can't come because she's having a spa day with her mom." Poppy rolled her eyes and made a silly face. Jane burst into laughter, which helped break the awkwardness.

Poppy turned left down the street that led to the beach. Poppy's hand appeared in front of Jane. She was twisting her shoulder to reach back, so much so that Jane thought she was going to dislocate her shoulder. Jane clasped her hand, and Poppy gave it a little squeeze.

"Thanks again for coming. I know you must be feeling quite nervous cause of them teasing you but I'm glad you came," she said.

Jane blinked. Poppy sounded really genuine. "Thank you for asking me to come!" Jane said.

"If you ever feel uncomfortable today, or if Jack is being a douche. Just tell me and we can just go home, ok?"

"Yeah, Jack has been a bit of a dick lately, but we'll look out for you." Nico gave Jane's shoulder a gentle tap. "I'm not sure why you're getting the wrath of his teasing… Maybe Jackie boy has a little crush," Nico added with a wink.

"Oh shut up Nico," Jane gave him a playful shove. "It'll be ok," she said, half to herself. Strangely, Poppy's words made Jane more nervous, not less. "But will do," she added. She smiled at Poppy as they come to a stop. Poppy gave her one last squeeze, before they hopped out of the car.

Taking her sneakers off to walk in the sand, Jane realized she hadn't been to a beach for years. She'd forgotten how much she loved it. She drew comfort from the thought and held tight to it as they trudged further down the beach.

After about five minutes of struggling through the sand, they made it to "the spot". Poppy told her this was where she and everyone else always hung out when they came to the beach. It was the first Jane had heard of this.

Nico started setting up a base for them. They had a couple of deck chairs, a mat laid out, and a Bluetooth speaker already blaring. Poppy dropped all her things dramatically and jumped up towards him.

Nico caught Poppy and they spun around. Most people their age would have either rolled their eyes or completely swooned. Jane just thought it was nice that they seemed to really, really like each other – maybe even love each other – but it was too early to call.

Jane dropped all her stuff on the mat with Poppy's and took a seat.

Poppy looked back at her. "Oh man, I'm sorry. PDA – whoops haha." Poppy went over to the cooler and opened it, grabbing a couple of sodas, handing one to Jane. "Here." She set up another deck chair and sat down next to Jane, while Nico finished setting up the rest.

Ten minutes later, their set-up looked pretty epic. Jane got out her brother's old Canon camera to take a few pictures. Before her brother went off to the army, he took the whole summer off to hang out with her, and one of the things he did was teach her how to use a camera. Ever since then, she'd fallen in love with every aspect of photography. Will still hadn't called her since he left, after a falling out with mom, she guesses he was still trying to process everything and live up to dad's legacy. She took a couple of snaps of the set-up and just the beach in general.

Nico peered over Jane's shoulder watching her play around with the settings. "Hey, can I have a look at your photos?"

Jane hadn't really shown many people her photography except for her family and Poppy. Maybe Poppy told him about her hobby.

"Sure," she said passing the camera back to him.

He looked at the screen, flicking through the pictures. "Whoa!"

"Is that a good whoa or a bad whoa..." Jane laughed nervously.

"Is that even a question? These are amazing! How'd you get so good at this? Seriously, people would pay to have these framed in their houses." He passed the camera back.

Jane grinned. "Thanks Nico, maybe I'll start looking into that as a career..."

Nico burst into laughter. "You haven't considered it before? Oh my goodness, Jane!" He playfully punched her in the shoulder.

Suddenly, a squeal rang out from her left. Lowering the camera, Jane watched Poppy run out to meet the rest of the group. She grabbed two of the girls, squeezing them both in a big hug.

Jane couldn't help but document the happiness in front of her. Poppy didn't wait for the boys to catch up, as she excitedly brought the girls over.

"Jane! Cool camera. Feel free to take as many snaps as you want to, huh Julie? Sarah? You don't mind? Jane's really talented, you know," said Poppy.

"Yeah, no worries," Sarah said. Julie nodded.

Jane couldn't help but giggle. Poppy's excitement was infectious.

Jane hopped up from her chair, giving them both a hug. Julie leaned in, tucking her strawberry-blonde hair behind her ears. Her face was caked in makeup, and Jane could see the strap of a bright pink bikini top under her white top. Sarah had tied her hair into a messy bun and was wearing a Nike tracksuit. She was part of the lacrosse team at school and must've just come from practice. Jane couldn't believe they still had to go to practices during the breaks! It would have been enough to make her quit the team.

The first time Jane had been introduced to them she had held out her hand for them to shake. They had both stared at it, and then glanced at each other. Jane had felt her stomach drop, knowing she'd just made things awkward.

She remembered catching Poppy's eye, and she had rushed over. She could remember Poppy's sentence word for word.

"Oh, silly Jane! We aren't big hand-shakers around here, are we? We like to exchange hugs." She pushed Jane toward the other girls. Jane fumbled, and then just went with it. She'd embraced the two girls, laughing, and they hugged her tight. She'd stepped back, and they all exchanged a smile. From then on that's how she greeted all the girls in her group.

Further up the beach, Nico walked towards the rest of the guys, giving them all a handshake-hug kind of thing. They all patted each other on the back a fair bit too. Jane felt like she was watching a nature documentary, observing the customs of a foreign species.

Poppy sat down next to her, perhaps sensing her nerves begin to rise. Jack, Sam, Tommy, and Lucas joined them. Before Jane could say hello, Jack cut in front of her.

"Hey! Poppy, you brought Jane along! Awesome, Nico was just talking about how good you are at photography."

Jane blinked. She wasn't used to Jack being this nice. He hadn't even called her "The Freak's Friend".

Jane smiled at him, appreciating the friendliness. It must have been the break from school putting him in a good mood.

Jane said a few quick hellos to the rest of the boys, then turned her attention back to the girls. They were chatting about the school dance. Jane couldn't believe they were planning their outfits this far ahead – the dance wasn't until the last week before summer break!

The boys set up a game, which Jane gathered was called "spike ball". She raised her camera and took a quick snap of them all. It was kind of cute, watching them concentrate so hard. Someone's hand hit her on the shoulder, jolting her and ruining the shot.

"Hey boys! Jane's got her camera out. Take your shirts off!" Sarah yelled. She tried a wolf whistle but ran out of breath.

They laughed at her poor attempt but obeyed her command and took their shirts off, even though a freezing wind was blowing. Julie, Sarah, and Poppy all squealed and whistled at them, hyping them up.

Poppy nudged Jane with her elbow. "Go on. Get snapping!"

"Ok, ok!" Jane blushed a little but kept shooting anyway.

Each one had their own stupid pose, which made her chuckle behind the lens. Goosebumps rose, covering their skin, as they tried to hide the fact that they were cold through the way they posed. The girls stripped to their swimsuits, letting out squeals of "I'm so cold," and "It's freezing!" and joined the boys. They all cuddled in together and Jane took another picture. They were all crazy. Hopefully they weren't thinking about taking a dip.

A thought dawned in the back of Jane's mind. Maybe she was just there as their photographer. She had been a part of their group for a while now, but they'd never invited her to the beach before. She shook the thought off, not wanting to ruin the moment.

"Jane! Set up a timer and join us!" Sam yelled.

"Yes, come on!" Poppy agreed.

Jane grabbed the cooler and made a little makeshift tripod. She set up the timer.

"And take off your clothes. Gotta be in your swimsuit!" Jack called out.

"Are you kidding? It's freezing! You guys are crazy!"

"Just do it! We are at the beach, aren't we?" Jack replied.

Jane felt shivers crawl up her back. She'd never been in a swimsuit around anyone else before, except family. They all looked eager to see what she was hiding underneath. Jane read all their faces, Jack's looking the greediest. Poppy was the only one displaying any concern.

Jane took a breath. Why not? She knew that having friends, some parts might make her uncomfortable. Even when Poppy asked her to come, the thought of being in a swimsuit had almost made her say no.

Jane sucked up the last bit of confidence she had left and quickly unzipped her Levi's. She threw her hoodie and thermal off to the side, then pressed the timer on the camera and ran towards the group.

She didn't look at any of their faces. She felt her cheeks heating up. She stood awkwardly next to Lucas. His gaze was on her, she could feel it.

Finally, she swallowed the last of her fear and looked up towards them. All of her friends had stunned expressions on their faces, except Poppy. Poppy gave her a thumbs up and a warm smile. The camera clicked and Jane made her way back to it.

"Another! We were all distracted," giggled Poppy.

Jane laughed too and reset the timer. This time, Lucas opened his arms for her to join the group. He pulled her in, his hand resting lightly on her shoulder. She couldn't help her shivering and leaned into him for warmth.

Jane placed her other hand on her hip, and they all looked towards the camera, smiling as it clicked. Before Jane could walk back to the camera, Poppy ran ahead and grabbed it.

"Is it the same as my camera?"

Jane opened her mouth to answer, but Poppy already had figured out the differences. She took a photo of Jane, then started hyping her up. Jane blushed.

Suddenly, a pair of arms wrapped around Jane's waist. She squealed, but Poppy just kept taking pictures. Then she felt Jack's mouth, right by her ear.

"What a surprise, Jane. We should've invited you to our beach trips a long time ago. You're hot for a freak's friend, that's for sure."

Jane grabbed his hands, yanking them off her waist.

"Wow, and here I was thinking you weren't such a dick after all. You seem to prove me wrong every time I get my hopes up."

Jack raised his hands, laughing at her. "Whoa, whoa, all I was saying is that maybe if you only hang with us, maybe we could revise your nickname."

"What? The nickname you gave me?" Jane didn't feel like holding back her anger anymore. He'd almost seen all of her and now he could hear her too.

He chuckled and scratched his head. "Hah, yeah sorry about that."

"Yeah right, you're sorry. You're a horrible human being. Did you know that? Oh no of course you didn't." She wrapped her arms around herself, trying to hold in her warmth.

"Wow." Jack looked around at the others, inviting them to laugh with him. "The Freak's Friend has some fire in her." He stepped towards Jane, getting too close. "She's smoking hot now."

Jane looked at Poppy and gestured for her to give back the camera. Jane knew exactly what she wanted to do with it. She pointed it at Jack's face and flipped him off in front of the lens. In the picture, all you could see was his shocked expression around her middle finger. Nico burst out laughing as Jane walked away with Poppy following her.

"Don't worry about him," Poppy said. "He's always been a dick."

Jane nodded, too shaken to say anything else right at that moment. They grabbed their clothes and put them back on. They got out their towels and laid them down on the sand, joining Sarah and Julie "sunbathing" while the rest got stuck into another game of spike ball.

Almost as if it knew they were waiting, the sun came out for a moment and beat down on Jane, but it wasn't the only thing that made her feel an uncomfortable heat.

7.

Jane

Throughout the rest of the week, Jane hung out with Poppy and the rest of the group. Sometimes it was just her and Poppy, but more often than not it was all of the girls or the group as a whole. They either went to the local park, the beach, or Poppy's house. She started to feel like she finally belonged somewhere.

Even though she had been a part of the group for some time, she'd still felt like she was on the edge – just Poppy's friend, rather than a core part of the group. Now, they had invited her into their group chat. It was the first she had heard of it, and she was kind of offended she hadn't been invited earlier. Poppy said they hadn't been able to find her. She supposed she did have an odd username, but it was a pretty poor excuse. Jane wasn't sure why they hadn't just asked her. She shrugged the thought off.

They had stopped calling her "The Freak's Friend" at least. She hoped it would stay that way once school started back up. The closer that day came, the more anxious she felt.

*

Her butterflies wouldn't settle. The pre-winter break had gone by in a blur, and it was the first day back. She'd been texting Poppy all morning. Poppy assured her that everything would be ok, and that surely Jack wouldn't pick on her. Jane found that difficult to believe.

She got all her things together and gave her shirt a quick iron. Her phone buzzed non-stop. She was starting to regret joining the group chat; they never stopped messaging. She never really messaged anything herself, unless someone was asking whether she was going to make it to one of their group hangs.

The buzzing finally came to a stop as she slipped on her shirt, rolling the sleeves up a little. She put on a plain pair of pants and a thick gray cardigan, then grabbed her bag and made her way towards the door. It was getting colder and colder with every new day that passed.

Jane nearly forgot her phone. Almost as if it predicted it was going to be forgotten, a notification came through, catching Jane's attention. For a split second, Jane thought that maybe she could still "accidentally" forget it, but she went and scooped it up anyway.

She made her way back to the door, then looked down at her notifications. Almost all of them were from the group chat. She would have to put it on do not disturb once at school.

Another message was from Poppy: SEE YOU AT SCHOOL!

Jane swiped away the notification, revealing another message. This time from Jack. After what had happened at the beach, it was no surprise he hadn't messaged her once over the break. But for some reason, he'd decided to today. Maybe it would just be a "see you at school" message like Poppy's, but Jane doubted it.

Jane took the last few steps out of her door, closing it behind her and locking it. Before she started down the porch steps, she tapped the message icon, opening it.

IF YOU WALK TO SCHOOL WITH THE FREAK, YOU'LL BE THE FREAK'S FRIEND AGAIN. YOUR CHOICE.

Her heart felt like it dropped into her stomach. She chewed on the words in the message, wanting to spit them back out. She didn't want to lose everything she'd gained over the break. She didn't want to be known as "The Freak's Friend" anymore. She swallowed, absorbing the message as she did.

Slipping her phone back into her pocket, she held her cardigan closer to her and continued down the steps. She looked towards Theo's house. She badly wanted to go over there, especially considering yesterday, the last day of their little break, he'd almost bumped into her when she hopped out of Poppy's car. He'd been heading out for a run, but tears brimmed in his eyes. He had looked so distressed.

She'd waited for him to return home to ask what was wrong, but the weather had taken a turn for the worse, so she headed inside to start dinner. She could have messaged but it didn't feel appropriate.

He was probably waiting for her, like he always was. He would be sitting on the edge of the stairs, all ready for her to knock at his door, then he would stand up and straighten out his clothes, take one last look in the mirror, sometimes fixing his hair before opening the door and joining her on the way to school. She didn't think he knew that she could see him go through his cute little routine before he opened the door. The more she thought about it, the harder it was to betray him.

It wasn't that big a deal, though, was it? It wasn't like he needed her to walk with him. He knew the way now and was perfectly capable of walking by himself. She didn't need to baby him, just because he had autism. Maybe the independence would be good for him!

Jane swallowed. Even as she thought this, she knew it was all an excuse.

Before she could let herself think about what a horrible person she was becoming, she turned on her heels, twisting in the other direction, making her way towards school.

About ten minutes later, Jane reached her school. She hadn't realized how much she and Theo must dawdle on the way to and from school. Normally, she would be arriving bang on bell time or just before. It felt strange to arrive earlier than normal.

She checked the group chat to see where they were all meeting before school – outside the common area, at this special place just for the senior students. They usually sat on the benches looking into a little garden. Thankfully the benches were under shelter from the drizzle that had started. She made her way over.

Someone was sitting on the bench already – one of the guys, though she couldn't see who. She prayed it would be anyone other than Jack, but as she got closer, he turned around and smirked at her. She joined him, sitting, waiting for the rest of the group to arrive.

"Wise choice, Jane. Wise choice," Jack murmured.

She almost replied with a snarky comment but held her tongue. Instead, she turned her back on him. He made her so mad.

"Aww, Janie… do you feel bad about leaving the poor helpless freak to walk to school all by himself?" Jack said in a cry-baby voice. How dare he call her "Janie"?

"Just drop it, would you? I listened to what you said, so just… just leave it. And he's not helpless…"

"Aw, sorry Janie. Did I hurt your feelings? Look on the bright side, you're not The Freak's Friend anymore."

"You started that Jack, but whatever." Jane didn't want to be there anymore. She didn't want to hang out with Jack. She stood up, having had enough, and turned away. She started walking, but his hand gripped her shoulder. He leaned in, whispering right into her ear. "You're mine now. You always have been."

For a moment, Jane shut down, completely forgetting how to function. When he let go, it felt like she restarted. She walked away, her steps stilted and awkward. She sped up, trying to get further away from him.

"If you go back, you'll regret it!" Jack shouted behind her, his words echoing.

Jane looked over her shoulder at Jack, but she kept walking, slamming into someone.

"Hey, hey, hey! Be careful, that's my girl you've just walked into…"

Jane recognized the voice, but everything felt floaty. She could still feel Jack's hand on her shoulder, his breath on her cheek as he whispered.

"Jane?" Nico waved his hand in front of her face.

Jane blinked. Poppy stood in front of her, books on the floor, where Jane had knocked them. "Oh, I'm sorry." She quickly stooped down, gathering Poppy's things. Poppy knelt next to her, helping.

"Jane? Are you ok?" Poppy's voice was gentle.

Jane sniffed, trying desperately not to cry. She handed Poppy the books and stood quickly. Nico and Poppy both stared at her, but they weren't mocking her. Both of their faces held sincere concern. It was exactly the type of thing that would make her cry more. Instead, she gave them a quick smile and squeezed past them.

"I'll see you in class," she said, leaving them clueless. She rushed toward the girls' bathroom.

Pushing through the door, Jane found the nearest stall. She locked herself inside it and put the toilet lid down, sitting on it. A sudden explosion of anger thundered through her. She hurled her bag at the stall's door. The crash echoed around the room, as she lay her head in her hands, resting her elbows on her knees.

Jane let out a raw, strangled scream, feeling too mad to cry. Why did some people have to be so sucky?

She lifted her head and looked up towards the ceiling. Why was she such a wimp? A no-good, peer-pressured wimp? She couldn't believe that she liked Jack once, what was wrong with her?

The bell rang, cutting through her thoughts like a sharp knife. Jane ran her hands down her face, trying to scrape away the last of the anger. She grabbed her bag and unlocked the stall door. Her face in the mirror wasn't something to be proud of – blurred eyeliner giving her panda eyes, and her skin was a blotchy red.

The bell rang again, drawing Jane out of her thoughts for a second time. It was the two-minute warning bell.

Jane gave her face one last gentle rub, and walked out of the bathroom, heading to her first class of the day, History.

*

Jane felt like she was moping around for the rest of the day, which technically she was. Usually, she hid her feelings under her mask better. Poppy could tell something was up. She asked Jane what was wrong a couple of times, but Jack was always there, listening.

"Nothing. I'm fine," Jane told her.

Poppy frowned, like she didn't believe her. Jane tried forcing a smile, but she could tell it didn't look convincing.

Poppy let it go, but Jane knew she'd probably message her about it that night. The rest of her friends had hardly noticed, though at one point she saw Tommy elbow Lucas.

"Stay out of Jane's way today, dude. Time of the month."

Lucas spluttered out a laugh, which he tried to cover up when he saw Jane looking.

Surprisingly, Jack didn't say another word to Jane all day… Still, she felt uneasy, like she'd stumbled into the wrong place, and didn't know how to escape.

On the bright side, at least no one had called her "The Freak's Friend".

*

As the school day came to an end, Jane said goodbye to her friends. Poppy gave her a comforting hug, and she started to walk home.

Not too far from her house, Jane heard shouts coming from Theo's place. It didn't sound happy. Maybe he'd had a bad day at school. Though, when Jane thought about it, she hadn't seen Theo once at school.

She stopped, gasping. He'd never made it to school. Maybe he hadn't been able to handle the change, and it was all her fault. She'd betrayed him, with no warning.

Looking up, she saw his screen door fly open, and he came running out. Sandra ran after him but stopped at the edge of their porch steps. She'd never be able to catch up with him.

Theo's dad came storming out too, yelling for Theo to come back. Sandra looked up at him, and he enclosed his arms around her, her shoulders shaking softly.

Theo saw Jane and made a beeline towards her. Not knowing what else to do, she raised her hand to give him a little wave. She cringed internally, knowing she was acting like nothing had happened… like none of it was her fault.

Theo suddenly changed directions, moving his eyes back to the horizon. He ran past her.

"I'm so sorry!" Jane yelled at his back.

He just kept running until he rounded the corner and Jane could no longer see him. Jane stared after him, then slowly turned back to her house. She gave a shy wave towards Theo's parents, still holding each other on their porch. They didn't return it, but perhaps they hadn't seen it. She jiggled her keys into the lock.

Once she was inside, Jane slammed the front door and rested back against it. A sob escaped her and then another, each one quaking through her.

What had she done?

8.

Theo

It was a perfectly good break, Theo thought. He didn't interact with anyone, really, but then again, he hardly ever did. He did message a friend from his old school, to see if they were free to hang, but unfortunately, they still had school. He spent most of his holiday in the garden, planting seeds, replanting flowers and other plants to create a perfect sanctuary for his butterfly friends. Theo loved butterflies; they made him feel calm. In his spare time, if he wasn't running, he tried to learn as much as he could about them. He would happily spend the rest of his life in his backyard. But then he wouldn't be able to see Jane.

He and Jane had walked together every day since he started attending her school, and he didn't have any reason to think that would change.

There were two things that had changed in his life recently, and Theo didn't think he could handle a third.

The first big change was that he'd joined the school's track team before school broke up for the week. That had been a big day.

He'd come home that night, still thinking about it. His mom had said later that she'd noticed he was unusually quiet, but she'd thought that maybe he was preparing himself for the change of the pre-winter break. A change to the school calendar was big, but not as big as joining the track team.

When they all sat down at the table and started eating that night, Theo couldn't hold his giddiness in. He was beyond excited to tell them what he had done. He remembered the exact moment his dad rested his hand on his quivering shoulder. It was 7:12 p.m.

"Are you alright, Theo?" his dad asked.

"Yes, what's wrong, love? You're scaring us," his mother continued.

59

"I have an announcement to make," Theo told his parents. Both sets of eyes were now on him, and he felt a little uncomfortable. His leg wouldn't stop bouncing. He took a deep breath and continued. "I did something at school today." He paused for effect. He had seen this done in his favorite TV show, Friends. In episode 15, season 9, at five minutes, thirty seconds, Joey had read out loud "long pause" on his script instead of pausing, which Theo made sure he didn't do. Friends always made Theo burst into laughter whenever he re-watched it.

"C'mon spit it out, son," his dad said. "Don't leave us waiting. You're scaring your mother."

"I joined the school's track team!" Theo said, as he raised his hands above his head in celebration.

Dad gave him a pat on the back while his mom squealed and covered her mouth in surprise. They were all happy.

The second change was one that he never saw coming. It happened on the last day of the pre-winter break. His mom called him for dinner, but instead of him being upstairs this time, he was in the garden planting a new plant his dad had bought him earlier that day. They all sat around the table, like they did every night, but this time it had felt different. Theo could sense the tension in the air. His parents were way too quiet – they were never quiet – and he couldn't handle it.

"Tell me what's going on!" Theo couldn't help but be blunt. His mom tried to soothe him by rubbing his shoulder, but he shrugged her off.

"I'm serious, what's going on?"

"Well..." his mom hesitated. She looked at Theo's dad. "You know how your father hasn't been around much lately? And he's gotten really into golf?"

"That was a lie, son," his father said.

Theo laughed to himself. "No, duh! I know I'm not Sherlock, but I already knew that, considering you don't have any golfing gear at all. And one time you even went to 'golf' wearing sweatpants and an old hoodie, so of course it's a lie."

His mom and dad reached for each other's hands. They both still had a guilty look in their eyes.

"That's true, son, but it doesn't explain why I've been so busy lately." His dad paused to scratch his head.

Theo watched him lower his hand. A light clump of his hair fell to the floor.

"No," Theo said. "No, no, no. You have cancer?" Theo practically yelled.

His mother covered her mouth. His father reached out to him, but Theo shrugged away. He bent down and grabbed the clump of his dad's hair and dropped it right in the middle of dinner.

"Theo!" They both yelled. His dad snatched up the hair, and his mom examined the dinner, plucking out stray hairs. They both huffed and puffed, but Theo just shook his head, not listening to them.

"Yes, Theo, you're right. I'm sick. However, there was no need to do that to the food. Your mom has been under a lot of stress lately, and she worked very hard on dinner tonight."

Theo didn't know what to say to that, so he didn't say anything. His mom and dad looked at each other.

"We know you must have questions, sweetheart..." his mom said, eventually. Theo did have questions, but there were too many of them. He stared at his feet. There were still a few hairs on the ground.

"I found out just before school started this year," his dad said. "I'm just starting radiation."

"That long! Is that why I had to change schools? You told me we couldn't afford it anymore. That's when you should've told me the truth, that you had to pay for your medical bills. Why'd you wait so long to tell me?" Theo couldn't stop staring at those hairs on the ground. "You should've told me from the start."

"We didn't know how you would handle it! You were already dealing with having to start a new school, Theo. Please don't be angry," his mom said.

"Don't be angry? Don't be angry? How could I not be angry about the potential death of my dad?" Theo pushed himself back from the table. His chair made a screeching sound.

He couldn't control how he felt. He needed to get out of there. He stood up, briskly walking towards the front door, and threw on a pair of sneakers.

"Son, son, wait. We're sorry. We didn't know what would be best. Please." Theo's dad ran after him. He grabbed his arm.

He did look ill, Theo thought. His eyes had a sickening numb look; his emotions barely showed through them. He looked tired.

"Stay," his dad said. "I know you might need to run right now, but please stay for your mother. We need you."

Theo felt a tear trickle down his cheek. Before it became a waterfall, he opened the door, pulling his arm from his dad's grasp and ran down the porch steps.

Theo sprinted down the footpath, almost crashing into Jane who was just getting out of Poppy's car. She stopped him short. They made direct eye contact.

He brushed away the tears that were beginning to overflow. He moved past her abruptly, but still gently so he knew he hadn't hurt her, and ran off down the street.

He heard his parents yell after him, asking him to come back, but all he could feel was Jane's eyes on his back. They – Mom, Dad, him – they weren't happy anymore.

*

On the first day of school after the break, Jane didn't come. She never knocked. She never said anything to Theo about not walking to school together. He was going to tell her everything that had happened last night and apologize for running past her.

Why did things have to change?

Theo couldn't go to school that day. Walking with Jane was one of the reasons why he'd stayed in school. He wasn't an idiot. He'd heard what people said about him, but walking with Jane was something that helped, even if nobody else knew it.

But she wasn't there that morning, without any warning. Theo had thought if she hadn't wanted to walk with him, she would have at least said something. But who was he kidding? Why had he thought she would walk over, look directly at him, and say "We aren't walking together anymore". She was too kind to do that… or maybe she was the opposite.

The change was too much for Theo. There had been too much change lately, and Theo could feel himself shutting down.

He couldn't go to school. He couldn't. He dropped his school bag on the stairs and kicked off his shoes. He sat down, hugging himself gently, rocking himself back and forward.

His mom came up behind him, pausing. He guessed she was looking at his bag and discarded shoes. He heard her sigh and make her way around him. She took a seat on the step below him.

"I'm sorry," she said. It was like she had no other words in her vocabulary.

Theo said nothing. His mind couldn't seem to form a sentence with all the words he felt. Without meaning to, he rocked more.

"C'mon," his mom said. "Up you get. Let's go to school. I'll drive you today."

She didn't understand that it was much bigger than that. It wasn't because he didn't want to walk alone. It was so much bigger than that. He rocked harder.

"Theo, can you try to explain to me how you feel?" His mom tried to get in his face, to stop him from completely shutting down. She'd done it to him his whole life. Theo found it more annoying than anything else. He knew he seemed a bit closed off to physical touch but, right now, all he felt like was a hug. He pushed her back.

"Don't."

"Don't what, Theo?"

"Get out of my face, Mom." He looked up at the exact moment shock crossed her face. "I know it used to help, but I'm getting older. I'm not a little kid anymore," he blurted out.

Instead of huddling into himself, He straightened up, still rocking. His mom stood, retreating down the rest of the steps.

"Sorry, I'm just... I don't know what to feel. I feel too much! All at once. I don't know what emotion to pick. I feel... I feel too much, ok?" A part of Theo felt angry, he knew that much, and his mom was getting the full blow of it.

"It's ok. Shh, honey, it's ok. You don't have to go in today," his mom said, her voice soothing.

Theo stood, suddenly, fists at his side. He stepped down the rest of the stairs and looked directly at her. She looked so timid, unsure of herself. Seeing her like that broke Theo. He started to cry. Sobs rattled out of him, and tears rolled down his cheeks.

He reached for her, as he used to do as a child. She grabbed hold of him, and they fell softly to the ground together.

"It's not ok! It's not fair, Mom," he said between sobs.

"What's not fair?"

"All of it! I didn't ask to be the way that I am. I didn't ask for Dad to get sick. And... and the only person I want to talk to, the only one that treats me normally is Jane, and she's not here. She's not here! When I needed her most, she didn't come."

That was it. Theo had finally let it out, and he felt exhausted. His mom's shirt was damp, but he didn't want her to let go.

It was clear she didn't know what to say. He curled into her, both of them rocking with his cries.

"I want to disappear, Mom. I want to disappear."

9.

Theo

After two days at home, and a lot of running, Theo finally made his way back to school. He didn't want to go, but what could he do? Not walking with Jane was bound to happen eventually. Well, that's what he'd been telling himself anyway.

Theo stepped out onto the porch and looked back into the house, waiting for his mom to appear with the car keys. He would be taking advantage of being driven to school for as long as possible. He heard her coming, so he took the remaining steps down.

He glanced up at her house – Jane's house.

He could see her walking down the sidewalk on her way to school, her back facing him. All he wanted to know now was why. He wished she could have just told him why.

He pivoted on his heels, turning away, and walked to the passenger door, waiting for his mom to unlock it. He could feel his body rocking slightly, out of habit. His mom finally came out, locking the front door behind her. She glanced Theo's way, worry stretching across her face. She unlocked the car, and they both hopped in.

After putting their seatbelts on, she looked Theo's way and patted his hand. He gave her a nod, and she started the car, making their way towards school.

"Now, honey, I can't pick you up from school because I have to pick Dad up after his radiation treatment," she said, as she came to a stop outside the school. "If you need me to come and get you before then, just message."

Theo gave a small grimace, before saying a quick thanks. His mom still looked worried. It wasn't helping him keep himself together, so he quickly undid his seatbelt, grabbed his bag, and got out. He looked both ways before crossing the road to enter the school grounds. Not once did he look back

65

towards his mom. He passed the school gate and headed towards the building.

Since he'd missed the first two days of back at school, Theo had to head to the office to grab all of his missed papers. He walked up to the office desk, already passing peers whispering his not-so-secret nickname.

Ms Wilson sat behind the desk, thankfully one of Theo's favorite office ladies. She already had the things he needed ready, everything stacked neatly in a clear plastic pocket.

"Thanks Ms Wilson." Theo started to walk away.

"Psst! Theo! Don't worry about them. They're just stupid kids, but you didn't hear that from me! If you do need to report anything though, you know where to find me." Ms Wilson whisper-yelled after him. She sat back down, sticking her head back into her work.

Theo opened the office door, looking back at her. Of course, he promptly walked into someone. Just his luck!

"Dude, watch where you're going, alright?" It was Nico. Jane's friend. Also, from the most popular group in school.

Theo quickly dipped his head. He crouched down to pick up his papers, which had flown out of the clear pocket. Nico joined him. Theo watched Nico's hands move, roughly grabbing the papers, compared to his own hands which delicately picked up a single piece of paper at a time, without wrinkling it.

Nico passed Theo the papers he'd gathered, and they both stood.

"Remember to look, next time, yeah?"

"Thanks, yeah, will do." Theo tried to go past, but Nico stopped him, his hand stretched out in front of Theo.

"Freak?" Nico's eye's bulged, as he realized what he'd just said. "Oh uh… I mean Theo, is it?"

"Yeah. That's me."

"Sorry dude, my bad. It's out of habit you know with Jack around and all. You're looking good."

Theo hesitated. He had no idea how to respond to that. "Thanks?" he said eventually. "Same to you?"

"Been training lately?"

"What?"

"For the track team I mean. I'm actually on it too." Nico changed his stance as he said that, as if trying to look more like a runner.

"Oh, yeah, right, yeah. I've been running lots. You?"

Nico grimaced. "Yeah, yeah not much yet. Haven't found the motivation really."

"It's not about motivation. It's about discipline… really." Theo added the "really" on to the end to sound more… human. Apparently sounding human required adding a lot of unnecessary words. At least that's what the counselor at his old school had seemed to think. It must have worked though, considering Nico laughed and shoved Theo's shoulder in a friendly gesture.

"Wow dude, you're right. Maybe we could train together? Anyway, I'll see you at training or around school. See ya!"

"Bye," Theo mumbled.

They walked past each other, Nico entering the office, and Theo walking out into the crowded hall. His first interaction of the day, and it went better than he thought it would have.

*

School was going far better than Theo was expecting. Maybe the people in his grade had decided to grow up during the break. He didn't really believe that could be true, but the thought had crossed his mind. He still hadn't seen Jane though. Maybe she'd be in his English class.

His day had started with Biology, then Calculus and Physical Education before lunch. After lunch, he would have Art, then English. He was also taking Horticulture, but he wouldn't have that until tomorrow.

Now, he had to get through lunch. Theo wondered whether he would still hate lunch most out of all his periods. It made him laugh, because lunch was usually the students' favorite time during school.

He walked out of the gym, fresh from a shower, and made his way towards his locker. It took him three minutes, fifty-five seconds, according to his watch, to get to his locker from the gym.

Once he reached his locker, he took his bag off his shoulders, unzipping it. He chucked his sports clothes in the locker and swapped out some books, then grabbed his lunch. He was vaguely aware he was rocking, but he was so used to it, he thought nothing of it.

Theo was just about finished sorting out his things when his locker slammed shut, just missing his fingers. He jumped back, startled, dropping his lunch.

Jack snickered, a nasty grin spreading across his face. Earlier in gym class they had done the beep test, otherwise known as "The Multi-Stage Fitness Test". The more it went on, the more of his classmates had to drop out. Towards the end of the test, it was just Jack and Theo running. Jack had looked near death. He was sweating profusely whereas Theo had a calm composure. He did love running after all.

He could tell Jack didn't want to give up, or rather, he didn't want Theo to beat him, but his legs gave up on him. He fell awkwardly to his rear end in the middle of the test.

Theo had looked at him, noticing the hatred spreading across his face. Theo continued doing the test, doing three more beeps until he also gave up. Theo wasn't surprised Jack had now decided to show him who's boss.

Theo looked down at the floor, his sandwich below him. He bent down to pick it up, but Jack stepped forward, his foot landing on it.

"Oh, whoops!" Jack said in an exaggerated voice. "Sorry, Freak."

Theo knew… he just knew something was going to happen today.

"Cat got your tongue too? So, you're a mute now as well?"

Theo thought if he replied that would give Jack the reaction he was looking for. He stood, straightening up, and adjusted his bag onto his shoulders. He wasn't sure what to do next.

"My bad?"

"I have something else in my locker. Can you move your hand… please?" Theo mumbled.

"Oh, yeah sure, Freak."

Theo opened his locker again, hesitating to put his hand in to grab something else out.

"Don't worry, I won't slam it again."

Theo hesitated, then reached into the locker. Jack slammed the door shut as hard as he could. Theo cried out as the metal edging dug into his wrist.

"Get off it! Jack, you're hurting me."

"Aw, I'm hurting you? Let's go run to Mommy, shall we?" Jack leaned on the locker door, like it was a game. Theo tried to shove him off, but Jack dodged him, keeping his weight on the door. Theo tried to pull the door open with his other hand, but he couldn't with his wrist pinned. The door cut into him.

His eyes darted around the hallway, watering with the pain. He spotted Jane.

"Jane!"

She looked around, but she didn't see him straight away.

Jack let go of the door suddenly. Theo pulled his wrist free, clutching it close to him. But Jack wasn't done yet. He shoved Theo into the lockers, his forearm pinning Theo in place.

Leaning in close, he whispered, "Don't ruin her life too. She isn't yours anymore."

"She never was," Theo said.

Jack pushed him harder into the lockers. "Also, if you ever beat me again in class, you're dead."

Theo heard a rush of feet and things dropping. The weight of Jack lifted off him. He slid to the ground, enveloping himself, rocking uncontrollably.

"Dude, what the heck? Leave him alone." Nico yelled at Jack.

"Oh really? Really, Nico? You're defending him? Are you a freak now too?"

"Dude, just chill!" Nico scratched his head, glancing down at Theo. "He's on the track team. We might actually have a chance to win this year, and…" Nico's voice petered out. He put his hands in his pockets, looking from Jack to Theo.

Jack snickered. "Pretty sad if you have to rely on The Freak to win."

Taking her bag off her shoulders, Jane quietly knelt down next to Theo. She placed her hand on his shoulder. Theo felt his rocking slow. Jane didn't need to say anything. She knew how to be calm and help him through his moments.

But this time, it felt different. Theo looked at her hand, then stared at her before shrugging her hand off his shoulder.

Her face changed, her mouth falling open, and her cheeks coloring. Theo had trouble reading her expression, but he could see it changing again. She pulled back from him, and looked away, her eyes filling. Was she sad? He hadn't wanted to make her sad.

"Jane, get up. We're going to lunch now," Jack said.

Theo didn't want her to leave. She looked up at Jack, then back at Theo. Nico looked back at Theo too, before walking away. Poppy paused looking towards Jane and Theo and then back towards Nico and Jack.

They were all looking at each other, no one thinking for themselves. Theo stared down at the ground. In that moment, he hated all of them.

"Theo…?"

Theo heard Jane's voice, but he didn't look at her. She hesitated, then stood up. Theo still didn't look up.

She took a step backwards, but then hovered forgetting her bag. Theo heard Poppy mumble "sorry". She grabbed Jane's bag for her, but he still couldn't look up. Everything was too loud and too bright. He was rocking again, he could tell.

Jane's shoes squeaked on the vinyl, as she turned away.

Theo didn't look up until their backs were facing him. He stood and started rocking again. He felt everyone's eyes on him. Trying to be as calm as he could, he grabbed all his things and headed away from his locker.

He went to his art class. Outside, it had clouded over letting a gloomy light come through the wall of windows. It was fine since the lights above him illuminated the whole room. There wasn't any new painting hanging up which there normally was.

He considered this to be his best option for lunch from now on. He sat at the table that was covered in dried paint and felt himself slowly slip away. He looked at his watch, noting he had twenty minutes left before his next period. Twenty minutes to completely lose himself. He cuddled into his knees, letting himself rock freely.

10.

Jane

The rest of the school day was like torture for Jane. She kept replaying what had happened over and over again, making herself feel sick. She felt consumed by his reaction to her. She had always been able to help him when he needed her to, but he had pushed her away.

He pushed her away.

How could she have been such an idiot! She couldn't help herself but fall into the peer-pressure hole this school had created. But that wasn't an excuse. She'd hurt him. She'd hurt the oldest friend she had and acted as if she'd forgotten him.

She couldn't handle this feeling anymore. Maybe it wasn't so bad being called "The Freak's Friend". Wait, no, who was she kidding? It was bad, but this was worse.

She felt numb. No other words could explain it.

When Theo pushed her away – shrugged her off – she'd just left him. She'd stood up, and walked away with Poppy, following Nico and Jack.

She'd grabbed her bag off Poppy and said a quick thanks before changing direction to go to the bathroom. Poppy clearly didn't know what to think. Jane knew Poppy was the one who helped her with making "friends" and she couldn't thank her enough for that, but she could feel Poppy's awkwardness around Theo. Jane thought maybe Poppy felt bad about drawing her away from Theo, but Jane was the one who'd decided to let Jack get to her. She just needed to be alone.

Entering the bathroom, Jane was shocked to see how busy it was. A bunch of girls were fixing their makeup and a couple of stalls were locked. Jane heard the bell ring, a warning bell to say students should make their way to their next class. The girls made their way out, shuffling past Jane.

She let them pass before picking a stall and closing the door behind her. She wasn't surprised she'd gravitated towards the

bathroom again. It was a safe place. She put the toilet seat lid down, like she had done many times before, and rested her head in her hands. She didn't know what she was doing.

The bell went off again, echoing throughout the school halls. She was officially late for her next class, Photography. It was her favorite class, but she didn't want to go.

Hopefully, she could slip out of school altogether, once everyone got settled. Jane would never usually think of skipping, but she couldn't stand being there any longer.

After ten minutes of waiting, Jane left the bathrooms. She made her way down the hall, trying to avoid the hall monitors. She saw some other students floating around, slowly making their way to their classes.

Finally, she reached the office. After the office, it was just the steps, and she'd be out of school. She couldn't let the receptionist see her. Unfortunately, the receptionist had eyes in the back of her head, and she could always catch people trying to leave. Jane stood thinking about her approach when someone bumped into her shoulder. It was Poppy.

"Where have you been? We have Photography now. I've been looking for you everywhere."

"Sorry, yeah, I just—"

"You don't look so good."

"I don't feel so good."

"Why are you standing here then?"

"I need to leave. I don't have a note."

"Oh." Both of the girls went quiet, not sure where to go next with their conversation. Jane felt a compelling need to show how thankful she was for Poppy. Poppy was always there, even if she didn't always understand her friendship with Theo.

"Poppy, thank you."

"You're welcome… for what?"

"You're one of my truest friends and I can't thank you enough for staying by me even with Jack being a dick. I just feel… I don't know." Jane blurted out, shrugging.

"I'm glad I did. Like truly I am. Don't tell anyone but I like you the best out of everyone." Poppy giggled, then surprised Jane by wrapping her in a hug.

Tears started to stream down Jane's cheeks; she couldn't help them.

"I know what we can do…" Poppy took a step back to look at Jane.

"What can we do, Poppy?"

"I can get you out of school."

Jane blinked at her. "And how are you going to do that?"

"Like this!" Poppy grabbed the bottom of her shirt, ripping it.

Jane gasped and reached for her to stop. "What did you do that for?!"

"Because the teacher sent me to the office to get a new shirt. Duh! I got caught on the door handle…?"

Jane laughed. Poppy was so extreme sometimes. Jane's eyes started to well up with tears again, but before she could say thanks, Poppy twirled her around and pushed her towards the stairs.

Jane looked back to see Poppy marching over to the office. The receptionist swiveled around in her chair, facing the door and window. Poppy leaped in front of her, mumbling something about how the teacher had told her to get a new shirt.

Jane held a hand over her mouth, barely containing her laughter. It looked like Poppy was trying to impersonate a three-year-old having a tantrum.

With one final look back at Poppy, Jane snuck downstairs, opening the door as quietly as she could. She walked, or rather ran, out of the school grounds.

Once she was safely away from the school, Jane slowed down. She kept laughing to herself, thinking about what Poppy had done for her. She pulled out her phone, and sent Poppy a quick message:

YOU'RE THE BEST! <3

She put her phone back in her pocket and hurried away before she got spotted.

*

Jane rushed up her porch steps, hearing a car approaching behind her. She knew her mom was working a double shift that day, and probably wouldn't get a chance to come home in between. Jane looked behind her and realized it was Sandra, Theo's mom, pulling up to their house.

Jane quickly ducked behind one of her porch chairs, hoping she hadn't been seen. She peeked out, watching Sandra walk around to the other side of the vehicle to help someone get out. It was Theo's dad, and he didn't look too good. He looked older, somehow, and there were bald spots in his hair.

Maybe he was sick. Jane felt her heart drop even further. Maybe that was why Theo had been so upset the last day of the break when he ran past her after she got out of Poppy's car. She remembered it clearly now. He had tried to hold in his tears, except he didn't know about the one that had already escaped.

She didn't move from her spot, tracking them as they went up to their steps and into their house.

Once they were inside, she slipped her keys out and bounced to her front door, unlocking it, and closing the door behind her. It was weird to be home early on a school day. The sun was higher in the sky, so it wasn't shining through the windows as much.

Jane hadn't eaten her lunch, so she dropped her bag on the couch as she walked past and made her way towards the kitchen. She boiled the kettle and grabbed a packet of noodles in a cup. She would have been embarrassed to eat these in front of her classmates, but right now, she was safe in the comfort of her own home. She then sat down on the couch, turning on her favorite comfort show, Friends.

*

Two episodes later, Jane was starting to feel better. She'd just clicked onto the next episode, when her phone rang. She paused the TV and rummaged through her bag to find it.

She didn't recognize the number. Cautiously, she swiped right and put it on speaker.

"Hello?"

"Jane?"

Jane suspected it was the school calling, but why would they call her number and not her mom's?

"Speaking."

"It's me – Will."

Jane gasped and dropped her phone, as she raised her hands to cover her mouth.

"Hello? Jane? Are you alright?"

Jane fumbled to pick up the phone. "Hi, yes, sorry. I dropped my phone. You just frightened me, you know?"

Jane hadn't heard from her brother in five years. He'd left to go to the army, feeling like it was his duty after their dad had died. He'd fought with their mom about it for months, and one day, he just packed up his stuff and walked out the door. He did it when their mom was at work, only saying goodbye to Jane. That had nearly killed their mom.

"Yeah, thought that might happen. I should call more often, huh?"

"Yeah, you should."

"… I just wanted to call you. To see if you were ok. To see if Mom's ok. I hope… I hope I didn't cause too many problems."

Jane felt tears brimming in her eyes. She had done so much crying lately, she felt like it was becoming an immediate response to everything.

"Would have been nice if you called sooner to ask that." Jane didn't care that she was being blunt.

"I know! And I'm sorry. I had to sort myself out, and I just couldn't handle it anymore."

"You left us. You left me! Mom cried for weeks and had panic attacks. She kept saying one day we were going to get

a call saying you were lying dead in the middle of nowhere, just like Dad!"

Will was silent for a moment. "I know, I shouldn't have left the way I did but—"

"No! No buts. You left me. We were in this together and you just left me to sort out everyone's crap. No one was here for me. I hardly see Mom anymore. She keeps working doubles, so I have to do everything. And I mean everything. I make sure she eats, that she has clothes to wear, and that she has nothing to worry about! And all she does is sleep." All Jane's pent-up anger was spilling. "You know she took most of the photo frames down, because she would see you and it would set her off again, so it's like you don't even exist anymore! So 'sorry' isn't good enough." Jane felt a weight she hadn't even known had been there lift off her, and it felt so good.

"Jane…" His voice halted, and Jane knew he didn't know how to reply. He tried to say something, but his voice broke off again. She heard a sniffle down the phone.

"You know Mom and I… it wasn't healthy," he said eventually. "I had to get out of there. It was like she was smothering me. I didn't know that would happen; I thought she'd be better if I left. I don't know what to say… I'm sorry. Can I do anything to help…?"

"I don't need your help."

"Don't be like that, Jane."

Jane could hear a crack in his voice. He felt as broken as she did, she realized. He finally understood how much he'd hurt her.

"No." Jane hung up. She threw her phone to the other side of the couch, grabbed a pillow, and screamed into it.

She couldn't believe she'd just exploded at her brother like that. Before today, she hadn't even been sure he was alive.

He was alive?!

She needed to ring him back. She pounced on her phone. Three rings later he picked up, but Jane didn't give him a chance to speak.

"I'm sorry! I'm sorry I said all that. I forgive you. I forgive you, Will! You're alive! That's all that matters. It's been so hard lately… but you're alive!" Jane laughed at herself, and she could hear his laughter in the background too. She'd missed him. She couldn't hold a grudge against her own brother, no matter how long he'd been gone for.

"Jane, you don't know how much that means… I'm sorry… I should have been there for you and… I don't know. I feel like crap."

"You can always make it up to me."

"Oh, yeah?" His voice held a laugh. "How so?"

"Come and visit. I need to see you."

There was a long silence. "Jane…" he started, but paused sounding like he was out of breath. Jane's hopes fell. "I can't right now."

"Why? What… Why are you even calling me, then?"

"I'm on a mission. I'm in Turkey. And if I'm honest, about a few hours ago I had a near-death experience which made me think about how much I missed you."

"What? Are you ok?"

"Jane—"

"What happened? Are you hurt?"

"Jane! Stop! I'm fine. I just couldn't believe how dumb I've been. I should've called you the first week into my training, but I was being stubborn, and now I realize how much of an idiot I've been."

"Yeah, you still are, aren't you?"

"Hey, hey, hey." Will chuckled. "Don't bully your older brother. But yeah, I think I might have some leave coming up, so I'll make a plan to come and visit, ok?"

A warm feeling bloomed in Jane's chest at the thought. "Yes, please! I'd love to see you." Jane hesitated, unsure whether to ask for anything else. "But Will, can you do me another favor?"

"Anything."

"Can you keep in contact this time? If you show up on my doorstep without even a hint, I'll punch you." Jane couldn't

help the grin spreading across her face. It was so broad; she was sure Will would know she was smiling.

"Whoa, whoa, whoa." Will laughed. "Someone seems a bit grumpy. Something up grumpella? But of course, I'll make sure to message and call whenever I can now."

"Did you really just make up a nickname for me? Grumpella, really? Grumpy and Cinderella? Wow."

"Of course," he said in between laughs. "Whatever you're grumpy about, I'm hoping it's not still me, and you should go sort it. It'll make you feel better. Trust me, I feel as high as a kite. I haven't been this happy since, since you know…"

Jane swallowed. "…I know. I love you."

"I love you too. See ya later."

And with that, he hung up. She felt so strange, not knowing what feelings to settle on. She had been on a roller coaster of emotions, but she was happy he had called. At least that was one good thing to come out of skipping the end of school.

His suggestion ran through her mind – go and sort it. How? Maybe she should just go over to Theo's house and talk to him – explain how she felt. He might understand… Or he might not, but it was worth a shot.

11.

Jane

Jane waited until an hour before dinner time. She was procrastinating going over. She was only going to wait until he got home, but when he walked past, he had looked up at her house with such a sour expression that she ducked out of view like a wimp.

She thought she would wait until he had cooled off, but now the sun was starting to go down, and she was still pacing back and forth just inside her front door. She grabbed the door handle with determination but let it go again without turning it. She had to find another reason to get outside.

She walked back into the kitchen, grabbing the kitchen garbage can which, to her surprise, did actually need to be emptied. She tied a knot in the bag, before picking it up and swinging the front door open. The outside trash can was just a few paces away. She stomped down the steps, threw the bag into the can and closed the lid. She paused. This was it.

She made her way down the sidewalk leading to Theo's house, almost turning around with every step. She had to at least say she was sorry, or something along those lines. It would make her feel better, even if he didn't forgive her.

She reached his porch steps and marched up them, arriving at his front door. She knocked two times lightly and then a third, finding strength in the last one. There was shuffling of feet and chairs inside – Sandra was approaching, she guessed. The doorknob jiggled and opened. Behind it was Theo's dad. Jane took a step back. Up close he looked even worse. She outwardly gasped and tried to cover it with her hand.

"It's alright dear." His voice was heavy and slow, like he was gasping for breath. "I know I look sick."

Jane could only nod. She felt heat rising behind her eyes, but she didn't want to cry.

**80**

"I've hit a bit of a rough patch," he continued, filling the silence. "Poor Sandra is exhausted; she's asleep. Anyway, I'm rambling. Can I help you, Jane?"

"Uh… yes. Sorry Mr Williams. I hope everything is ok…"

"Call me Troy, Jane."

Jane nodded. She almost turned and ran, but she had come this far. "I was wondering whether I could speak with Theo?"

A look passed over Troy's face, and he glanced towards the back of the house. "Theo might be busy. He's out in the garden, but I can see if he has a spare moment." Troy began to turn away when he paused and turned back. "Sorry to be nosy Jane, but has your mom been home recently? Haven't seen her car in a while."

Jane gave an awkward laugh. "She's working doubles at the hospital at the moment, so she just comes home to sleep, eat, and change when she can."

Jane wasn't lying, but she wasn't telling the whole truth either. Her mom had been working double shifts, but she hadn't come home in a while. She was sleeping at the hospital. Jane hoped she was eating there too, but she couldn't be sure.

"Ah, ok." Troy hesitated. "It's just… I was at the hospital today and didn't see her there."

Jane felt her heart drop, not for the first time that day. What did he mean? She covered her puzzled look with a grimace.

"Maybe she was taking a nap in the staff room or something? The hospital is pretty understaffed." Even as she said it, Jane couldn't avoid the uneasy feeling creeping over her. She shook her head, brushing it away. "Anyway Sir, could I talk to Theo, please? It's important."

He hesitated, then smiled and stood aside, gesturing for Jane to come in.

Jane took a shaky step in and then a few more. Mr Williams closed the door behind her.

"The garden is this way." He led her through the living room and then into the kitchen. Jane had never been in Theo's house before. It was nice. Cosy.

Mr Williams gestured to a door, leading to the backyard.

"Thanks, Mr Williams, I hope you feel better soon!"

"Call me Troy." He winked and gave Jane's shoulder a little squeeze before walking away. Jane's father used to do that too.

Jane inhaled sharply and opened the door.

"Look at these," Theo said, as she did. "We planted these a month ago and they're just starting to open their bulbs. I wonder what butterfly will land on them."

He sounded so excited and so happy. Jane looked around. He'd turned the whole garden into a butterfly sanctuary. She suspected it was a sanctuary for him too.

She moved forward and stepped onto the stone path. "Those are really cool, Theo."

His head whipped up, not expecting it to be her. He stood, staunch. Jane hadn't noticed before how tall he was. She guessed she still saw him as the kid he'd been when they used to play together. She took a moment to really look at him now. His facial features were more defined, his jawline sharp. Freckles, from being outside in the sun, danced across his cheeks. Janes eyes traced down to his broad shoulders. She hadn't noticed them before either. Her heart swooned, and not just from his looks. She remembered how much she liked listening to him on their walks home and the times they'd laughed together. She forced her eyes back up, focusing on the reason she was here.

"Why are you here?" Theo asked.

Jane's mouth felt dry. "I just wanted to say how sorry I am."

"You shouldn't be here." Theo's eyes flicked away from her. "This is my home. This is where I'm most comfortable."

Jane nodded. "Yeah, you're right, but I didn't know where else to talk to you."

"How about at school?" He threw the snarky reply in her face.

Jane took a step back. "Look… I know what I've done, and I have no excuses. I just wanted to come here and tell you

what a mistake it was. I'm sorry and I hope you'll forgive me."

Theo stared at her for a moment. "Will you walk to school with me, then? Will you speak to me at school? Or are you going to start calling me 'The Freak' too? I'm not oblivious, Jane."

Jane shook her head. "So you know what I was called too then?"

Theo ignored this. Stepping forward, he intruded her bubble. "What does Jack have over you?"

Jane swallowed. The memory of Jack's fingers biting into her shoulder washed over her. His threatening words echoed in her ear. "Nothing," she said quickly. "Nothing, it's not like that, it's just—"

"It's just what, Jane? It's what?" He stepped forward again. Jane took a step back but stopped when she felt the stone path beneath her feet turn to dirt, a flower brushing up against her leg.

"I'm sorry, ok? I'm sorry." She wanted to say something else – something more meaningful – but there was nothing. Nothing except sorry.

"I trusted you." Theo took another step forward, their bubbles becoming one. They stared at each other for a moment. His eyes were hard, almost emotionless. "I trusted you," he said again.

Jane couldn't believe she'd thought this conversation might go differently. Who was she kidding? Of course, he wouldn't forgive her. The realization hit her like a punch to the chest. She couldn't help it, she started to cry. She felt herself falling back, stumbling on the edge of the path. Theo grabbed her forearm, steadying her.

Why had she only just realized what she was missing? She tugged her arm out of his grip.

"I'm so sorry," she said again. She turned away, running through his house without looking back.

Theo's dad yelled her name, trying to stop her. Jane acted like she couldn't hear him. She whipped open the front door and rushed down the steps.

Her vision blurred, and her head pounded, as she ran home. She threw open her front door and locked it behind her.

She took the stairs two at a time up to her room. She buried herself under her pillows and blankets, too tired to cry anymore.

Exhausted, and feeling alone, Jane lay there with her troubles weighing her down, making it impossible to resist the only thing that might make her feel better – sleep. She gave in. She felt the warmth that it brought wrapping around her, holding her tight and plunging her into a familiar abyss.

12.


Jane


A day or two had passed and nothing changed except the weather. It was becoming more and more like winter every day even though there was still a month of fall left.

Jane had only seen Theo a few times at school. At least they had one class together, Jane thought, as she took her seat in English class.

He sat toward the front of the room. She watched his movements, jagged and unsure of himself. Her heart pulled for him. She still felt guilty, as she replayed their conversation over and over. His last words to her echoed in her head, "I trusted you".

A book slammed down next to Jane, making her jump so high, she almost missed her chair when she came back down. Her English teacher, Mr Thompson, stared down at her. He had always been kind of a dick.

"Do you know why Shakespeare writes the way he does Jane?" he asked.

Looking back down at her notes, Jane noticed she hadn't written anything the whole lesson. She stared around the class cluelessly.

"Jane?"

She hesitated and blurted out an answer on the spot. "To be different… also back then he probably grew up being taught to speak that way, so he wrote that way too…" Jane trailed off.

Mr Thompson looked annoyed, but slightly surprised at the same time. "You're not completely wrong."

"Sorry, Sir."

"Start listening and maybe make the occasional note, if you can bring yourself to. I don't know where you went, but we do not daydream in this class!" He picked up the book he'd slammed down on her desk and stormed back up to the front.

Jane grabbed her pen and straightened her paper. When she looked up, Theo stared back at her. His gaze filled with worry, but when Jane met his eye, he turned it off, looking back at the whiteboard. His shoulders squared up, and he rolled them back, trying to relax.

A wadded-up piece of paper hit Jane's back. She turned around to see Jack waving at her like a dork. He pointed down to where it had fallen. If Mr Thompson saw that they were passing notes – or rather, that Jack was – it would be the end of both of them.

Jane dropped her pen purposely and leaned down to pick up both the pen and the paper. Un-scrunching it, she saw Jack had scribbled a drawing of her and a dream bubble with an inappropriate picture inside it. Underneath were the words "Daydreamer Jane".

She scrunched the paper back up and chucked it to the side. She'd pick it up later when class finished, but right now, she didn't want it anywhere near her. She was not going to give Jack the reaction he wanted. She would act like it simply never happened. Jane put her head down and tried to focus on what Mr Thompson was saying. She caught herself drifting back to where Theo was sitting. They made eye contact when he turned his head to look back, as if he was checking on her. Jane looked back down to her empty paper and decided to finally open her ears and take some notes.

*

Lunch finally arrived, and Jane picked up the note as she walked out of class, heading towards her locker. She threw it in a nearby trash can. She could feel Jack following her, and she just couldn't be bothered with him. He bumped into her, giving her a dirty look, then put his arm around her shoulder. She tried to shrug him off, but he was like one of those annoying flies that always comes back. She reached her locker and tried again, unsuccessfully, to shrug him off.

"What were you daydreaming about?" He leered at her. "Bet I could guess."

"No."

"Yes."

She sighed. "Jack, don't be annoying."

"Too busy dreaming about your lover boy in the middle of class?"

"What? No. Who?"

"You know… The Freak."

Jane frowned. "Don't call him that; he has a name."

"You did too."

Jane looked him dead in the eyes. He couldn't be serious. She took a step forward, purposely landing on his foot with all her weight. He yelped, and she used the moment to slam her locker door shut, making him jump.

She walked away, but it didn't take him long to recover. He grabbed her arm, holding it tight, and whispered into her ear.

"You can't just do that."

A threat, another one. Jane tugged her arm from his grip and turned around to face him.

"Stop acting like this. It's immature and you're a bully."

He shoved Jane back into a locker, both hands now pressing firmly on her shoulders. He got in her face, and Jane tried to turn hers away. They were practically breathing in the same air. Jane squirmed, trying to get out from under his grasp, but he just pushed harder in return. Her eyes darted around the hallway, trying to get someone's attention. No one looked her way; no one wanted to get involved.

"You can't talk to me like that," Jack whisper-yelled at her. Some of his spit landed on her cheek.

"You're hurting me. Jack, please get off." Jane's voice had turned to a whimper.

Jack smiled, pushing harder. "You want me to stop? Then listen closely. Stop defending The Freak."

"Stop calling him names! It's not his fault he's—"

"Shut up! If you want to survive in this school, you follow my rules, got it?"

Jane didn't answer. She didn't even nod, which she could see wound him up even more.

He looked around the hall, his eyes dancing from student to student. He caught a glimpse of someone coming round the corner and let go of Jane's shoulders. Her hands instinctively flew to them, rubbing her bruised skin.

Jack grabbed her around the waist with one arm, pulling her in close. His other hand curled around her jawline, hoisting his onto hers. He kissed her forcefully, as Jane tried to push him off. All that did was make him tighten his grip.

"Yooooo, I had a feeling dude!" Tommy's voice rang out from down the hallway. A chorus of wolf whistles and laughter went up.

Jane felt panic rising, and bile formed in her mouth. She couldn't get him off. She lifted her foot and brought it down on his, the same one she'd stood on earlier.

He shrieked, his face jerking away from hers. He loosened his grip on Jane and one hand reached down to clutch his foot.

Jane turned to see Tommy, Lucas, Julie, and Poppy rushing towards them.

"What the hell, Jane?!" Lucas yelled.

Julie and the guys went straight to Jack's aid. Jane grabbed his hand which still gripped her waist and twisted his index finger the wrong way. He cried out, clutching his hand to his chest.

Julie flashed Jane an annoyed look and turned to inspect Jack's hand. Poppy stared at Jane, shock and confusion showing. Then, she snapped into action.

"Come on." She grabbed Jane's hand, trying to whisk her out of the situation.

Jane shook her head, holding her ground. She nudged Julie to the side and looked directly at Jack. "Don't ever touch me again!"

Julie, Tommy, and Lucas crowded around Jack, helping him stand. "I don't understand… I just kissed her." Jack acted like a kitten, and the others fawned over him.

"Come on, Jane," Poppy said again. She tugged on Jane's hand, and this time, Jane let Poppy lead her away.

*

They entered the gym and sat down on the bleachers. Jane's whole body shook. She pressed her hands to the sides of her face, as if that would stop it. There was a game in progress, but all Jane saw was the blur of people moving, disconnected voices, and shouts accompanying it.

Poppy beckoned to Nico. He came over, calling a timeout on the game. He was sweating heavily and Jane cringed away, thinking of the feeling of Jack's skin against hers.

"Hey, babe." He reached over and gave Poppy a quick peck on the cheek. "Hey, Jane…" He looked between the two of them, obviously realizing something wasn't right. "Are you ok?" He dropped into a seat beside them.

"No." Poppy shook her head, her voice tight. "Jack just kissed Jane."

"Whoa, nice one, Jane!" Nico grinned at Jane, then his expression changed, taking in her demeanor.

Poppy squeezed his hand. "No, not like that, babe. We were coming down the hall to… ya know, meet where we always meet for lunch… when Jack had her pushed up against a locker. Like… like he was forcing himself onto her…" She paused, swallowing, and looked at Jane. Nico did the same.

Jane ran her hands down her face. Somehow, she felt both hot and cold at the same time. "He was talking crap about Theo again, and…" She shook her head. "I just wanted to stand up to him for once."

Nico reached over, grasping her shoulder. Jane flinched, whimpering a little as he touched her injured skin.

"Sorry." Nico let go. He and Poppy exchanged glances.

Jane swallowed, her throat dry. "I don't know. I must've overstepped a line because he pushed me into the lockers and wouldn't get off. He threatened me."

"Threatened you? Like he said he'd hurt you?" Nico frowned.

"He did hurt me." Jane stretched the neck hole of her shirt to show her shoulder. A red mark in the shape of a handprint covered her clavicle. The finger marks were starting to turn blue, the bruise forming as they spoke.

Poppy gasped and Nico grabbed her hand.

"That's not ok. We need to report him or something!" Poppy reached out as if to hug Jane, and then stopped, thinking better of it.

"There's no point." Nico shook his head, his jaw clenching in frustration. "He could get away with murder if he wanted. His dad basically owns the school council. It would properly damage you, Jane, more than it would him. His mommy and daddy can just buy their way out of the trouble he causes."

"Maybe…Nico, could you talk to him?"

"Talk to him?" Nico spluttered out a humorless laugh. "He doesn't listen to anyone, babe. Not me, not his friends, not anyone. He's the boss, and he just tried to make that clear to Jane… no offense Jane."

Jane shook her head. "Don't worry about it." She didn't really care anymore.

"Do you think he kissed you, so we wouldn't see what he was doing?" Poppy asked.

Jane had almost forgotten about the kiss. A kiss, taken away from her just like that. "Yeah, I suppose that was it. It was panicked. I didn't know what he was going to do next."

"Man, that's just messed up," Nico said softly. Poppy reached over, and gave her a gentle, somber hug.

"It's ok. I'll be ok." Jane gave them a smile to try and reassure them. It seemed to have the opposite effect.

"I'll make sure…" Nico started, then stopped himself as Poppy squeezed his arm. "We'll make sure you're never alone with him again."

Poppy nodded, confirming she would be there for Jane too.

"He's just a bully, but thanks, that means a lot." Jane grabbed Poppy's hand and gave it a little squeeze.

Nico gave Poppy a quick peck before returning to his basketball game, subbing on for someone else. Jane didn't feel like leaving, so she scooched over and leaned against Poppy. All her strength had diminished. She should have expected Jack to lash out physically at some point.

Ever since her brother had called Jane, and convinced her to go over and see Theo, she'd felt this need to stand up for him too. She knew it was the right thing to do – what she honestly wanted to do – but with Jack around, it was bound to get her into trouble.

Getting comfortable, Jane rested her head on Poppy's shoulder. She felt Poppy glance down.

Poppy radiated sympathy, bordering on pity. Jane pretended not to notice. She felt it coming from Nico too, as he glanced over. At least the two of them cared.

13.

Theo

Theo wished he had acted differently when Jane came to apologize. Seeing her like that had torn him apart. She always seemed so put together, nothing really seeming to bother her. Now, he'd seen her broken. He felt the same way.

In English class, he couldn't stop himself from looking back at her, but he made no move to go and talk to her. He couldn't if she was still friends with those assholes.

After class, he probably could only recall one-third of the material. Normally, he was pretty onto it during classes, never getting distracted, but lately, he couldn't help but be the opposite. So many things had changed, and it was still catching up to him.

He was one of the last students to leave, and if he was being honest with himself, it was because he wanted to follow Jane out, maybe talk to her on their way to their lockers. But he was too late. When he turned the corner, he saw Jack's arm around her shoulders. Jane's reaction gave him a little glimpse of hope. She shrugged Jack off, giving him an annoyed look.

Theo walked slowly behind them, glancing their way every now and again. They were nearly at her locker when Jane shrugged Jack off again.

Theo brushed past both of them and didn't look back. Down the hall he watched bustling students make their way towards their lockers. A slam echoed out behind him.

Around him, other students whipped their heads toward the noise, a few jumping, startled. Theo kept walking. He knew where the noise came from, the memory of the door closing on his wrist fresh in his mind.

He did think about going back to see if Jane was ok, but that might've made things worse for her. He just kept walking, ignoring the feeling of something or someone that was pulling him back.

92

*

School had finally finished for the day. Theo made his way out of his last class and across the school field towards the gate. He'd gotten used to walking alone, but he still wished things would go back to how they were before. Jane leaving him, and his dad's cancer, had thrown him off. They devoured his thoughts. Any spare moment he had was eaten away by overthinking.

His dad had gotten worse and he looked so weak. It never took Theo long to spiral down the path of what could happen to him. He could feel himself getting agitated, thinking of all the worst-case scenarios.

He decided to run the rest of the way home, and maybe also go for a proper run later on. His feet hitting the pavement, over and over, always settled his thoughts. It couldn't stop the overthinking completely, but it could quiet his head for a while.

Not far from his home, he saw a girl up ahead. He couldn't see her face, but her shoulders jolted gently, as if she were coughing or crying. He thought about jogging over to see if she was ok, but he had enough problems of his own.

The girl turned towards Jane's house. Of course, it was Jane. He felt like such an idiot now for not having recognized her. His heart wrenched for her, but didn't she have everything she wanted?

He quickly passed her house and jogged up his steps. Dropping his bag next to the stairs, he made his way through the kitchen and out to his little backyard sanctuary. It wasn't really much of a sanctuary anymore, since the butterflies had gone into hibernation. It was getting too cold for them now.

His garden looked a bit sad. He hadn't paid much attention to it lately. Every time he came out here, it made him feel sick. He and his dad had taken years to perfect it, but his dad was too weak to come out anymore.

The fight he'd had with Jane didn't help the atmosphere out there either. He gave his head a little shake. There he went again, overthinking.

He jumped over a few mud spots, passing all his neglected plants, and went to the only one that was still thriving. It was a singular purple anemone. Anemones loved the fall chill, but Theo knew it would get colder soon. That would be the end of this little flower's life if he left it there.

He ran back to the kitchen, grabbing out a pair of scissors. His mom stared at him, puzzled, but she didn't say anything.

He carefully cut the end of the stem and then went back inside. He quickly changed into some running gear, chucked some shoes on, grabbed his headphones, and said a quick goodbye to his mom. All the while, keeping the anemone close by. His mom chuckled to herself, but he wasn't sure why.

Theo walked down his porch steps, then crossed over to Jane's house. He wasn't sure how to approach what he wanted to do. Should he knock and hand her the flower when she answered? In the end, he decided it would be best to leave it at her front door for her to find. He didn't think it was the right time to talk to her yet.

He walked up to her porch steps and placed it in front of her door. He knocked twice and ran back down the steps, jogging off before she could answer.

*

Jane heard two taps at the door. She wasn't expecting anyone and wasn't sure she wanted to see anyone either.

She put her schoolbooks to the side and swung her legs off the couch. She peeked out, before she completely opened the door. An empty porch greeted her.

She looked from side to side. Still nothing. Glancing down, she finally saw what had been left for her – a flower.

She crouched, unsure how to approach it, as if it would bite.

The flower was a delicate purple anemone. The deep purples gave off a calm but mysterious vibe. Instinctively she looked towards Theo's house, but there was no movement from behind his curtains.

Picking up the anemone, she stepped back inside and closed the door. She grabbed a little vase out of one of the top kitchen cupboards, and popped the anemone in, filling it with water.

She carried it upstairs carefully. In her bedroom, she placed it on her window sill. She hoped it was from Theo, so she put it where he could hopefully see it from his own house.

The gift made her feel less cold, less numb, despite what had happened that day. Strange how the flower was something so little, but it felt so meaningful.

14.


Jane


A week later, Theo still hadn't spoken to her. She suspected the flower was from him – him trying to apologize in his way. At least, she hoped it was.

She had only seen him a few times at school. He always looked busy, like nothing was going to stop him from whatever it was he was doing. She hoped one night she would see him looking up towards her bedroom window, spotting the anemone he'd given her. Over the past few days, the anemone had opened wider, looking more alive than ever. Its oval-shaped petals stretching out, and the purples looking more vibrant. The color pulled Jane in. It wouldn't last long like that, though. The thought saddened Jane because the chances of him spotting it like it was now seemed slim. She hadn't seen much of him at home either. He was never out in the garden, even though that had always been where he seemed to live most of his life. The garden wasn't looking great either, which worried her.

She had seen him walk past two afternoons that week though. It had been quite late, and he'd had all his running gear on. She guessed the track team had started training. She use to see him in his garden almost every afternoon, but ever since the flower had shown up outside her door, she hadn't seen him in his garden once.

Jack hadn't done anything else to her. Perhaps he knew he'd gone too far and had taken a step back. He hadn't apologized, and Jane wasn't holding her breath. She knew he never would.

Poppy and Nico kept their promise – one of them was almost always with her at school. It made her feel like a nuisance, but she still appreciated them. Poppy had assured her she wasn't a burden, and Jane couldn't be more thankful that she had two real friends. Even so, she still felt like something was missing.

It was Saturday morning and Jane had a ton of homework to catch up on. Standing up from the bed, she pushed her curtains aside. It was a perfect fall day. A little frost covered the grass, but the sky was cloudless.

She walked downstairs and heard her mother in the kitchen. How strange. Her mom had worked the night shift after their quick dinner together, so Jane had thought her mom would still be asleep.

Jane crept around to the kitchen island, trying not to make a sound. Her mom sang quietly to herself, her back to Jane. Jane found herself smiling at her mother, her beautiful loving mother.

Her mom sang an old Elvis Presley song, one of her dad's favorites. Jane knew almost every word, and so did her mom. Jane joined in, softly singing along with her mom. Her mom whipped around. Shock showed on her face for a moment, then tears brimmed in her eyes.

Jane went to her mother, hugging her tight. Her mom's body shook gently. Jane reached behind her and took the pan of bacon off the heat as it started to burn. Her mom didn't register it, and Jane returned her hands to her mother's back, holding her tight. It had been a while since her mom had had a good cry, and Jane made no move to stop her. She knew that it was better out than in, something she needed to practice herself. Her mom squeezed her tighter and then she let go. She rubbed at her eyes smudging her mascara.

"I was just thinking about Dad and Will... They loved bacon for breakfast, and it just set me off." She laughed and Jane hugged her again. "It was this time of year when we would always have bacon for breakfast. Just something about the fall air always calls for a hot breakfast." She looked up, meeting Jane's eye. "I just miss him, you know? I want to hug my boy."

Jane hesitated, biting her lip. "Mom, can I tell you something?"

"Anything, yes, please honey."

"Promise you won't get mad..."

Her mother swallowed, worry tightening her features, but she nodded, firmly agreeing.

"Will called me," Jane said in a rush.

Her mom froze, then let go of Jane, stepping back. Shock crossed her face, a hint of betrayal following it.

Jane stepped towards her, not letting her mother pull away. "Mom, no, listen. It was a few weeks ago, and he didn't know what to say to you so he thought it would be better if he came in person first for you."

"And you're only just telling me, Jane Lilibet Davidson?"

Jane shook her head. "I didn't know whether you'd want to know. You never talk about him, and you took all his pictures down."

"Of course I want to know! He's my son!"

"Mom, you said you wouldn't get mad." Jane swallowed, her voice straining. "Please, I'm sorry."

"How could I not get mad about this, Jane?" Her mom stepped away again, backing into the benchtop. Jane felt like her mother was trying to get as far away from her as possible.

"Mom, please, I didn't know. He asked me not to."

"Oh, did he now?"

"Yes, but he had his reasons, ok? Just listen to me!"

Her mother made a noise in her throat. "And here I am cooking you bacon, trying to be a good mother, while you keep my son from me! You didn't think to tell me he's alive?"

"Mom, please—"

"No, Jane! You can't keep that from me. What, is Dad alive now too?"

"Mom, just—"

"I can't believe you!"

"JUST LET ME TALK!" Jane yelled.

There was a silence. Jane's mother looked like Jane had slapped her. Before Jane could even start, her mother walked away. Jane grabbed her wrist, trying to stop her, but her mother just dragged her, Jane's socked feet slipping on the wooden floor. Her mother twisted her wrist from Jane's

grasp. She ran into the bathroom, slamming the door behind her.

"Mom, please let me in! I'm sorry. Mom, please—" Jane thumped her hands against the door. There was no response from inside.

Jane leaned back against the door, sliding down it until she was sitting on the floor. Her mother sniffled from inside. At least her mother couldn't run away now. She would have to listen.

"So, about maybe three weeks ago, he called me. He had his reasons too, but man was I mad. I hung up on him, Mom." Jane laughed at the memory. "Then I called him back because I realized how silly I was being. He told me why he never called. He said he knows he's been selfish and not a very good brother or son at all. But he had a near miss, and… I guess things just hit him. He thought he had to hold up Dad's legacy, and that you would never understand, but I think he was just scared about how you would react." Jane paused, listening, waiting for a reply. Still nothing. She wiped at her eyes to stop the tears from running before continuing. "I miss him, Mom, and… and I miss you. You're never here. Physically or mentally. I went over to Theo's the other day, and Mr Williams opened the door. He asked about you since he didn't see you at the hospital… You were working a double that night too. Were you even there? I have school on my shoulders, and then I come home and keep the house clean and worry about whether you are eating or taking care of yourself. And now I think about whether you're even at work. It's not like I can ask you when you're home – you're always asleep. We never talk anymore." Tears choked Jane's words, so she wasn't even sure her mom could understand what she was saying. "When I found you this morning, I felt transported back to how it used to be. I know it must be hard for you, paying for the house, food, my school and everything, but… I need you too."

Jane's voice petered out into sobs. She let herself cry, the sound echoing around her. Then the door lock clicked, and her mom opened it slowly. Jane fell backwards, as the door disappeared behind her. She landed in her mother's lap, staring up at her face.

"I miss you, Mom," she whispered.

Her mom grabbed her, both of them sobbing uncontrollably.

"I'm so sorry, Jane," her mom said through her tears. "I don't know what to do. I'm just so sad."

"Shh, shhh, it's ok," Jane said, so used to comforting her mother, the words came out automatically.

They stayed connected like that on the bathroom floor for the next five minutes. Once Jane's mom finally got herself under control, she looked at Jane straight.

"I've been a terrible mother. It's true, I'm not always working doubles. More often than not, I am though. I have been seeing a grief counselor and spending time at a bar... I promise I'm going to try more from now on. It hasn't been fair on you."

"What do you mean? Why didn't you tell me?" Jane sat up, leaning away from her mom.

"I don't know? It was just easier to say I was working a double."

"Mom, that's not good enough. I could have gone with you. And a bar? Seriously?"

"I'm sorry, Jane, but you don't know how it feels to lose a husband!"

"You don't know how it feels to lose a dad! Not yet anyway – Grandad is still alive."

"Don't you dare say that."

"I just wished you'd told me." Jane felt betrayed. She no longer wished she'd brought up Will earlier.

"I don't know honey... I'm sorry, ok?"

"If you want to be a better mother, you need to tell me these things, instead of letting me assume. For all I knew, you were out with some guy hooking up!" Jane's anger boiled up. Her mother gasped, and a slap rang through Jane's ears as her

mother's hand struck her cheek. It was now Jane's turn to gasp. Her mom's eyes went wide with surprise.

"Oh no! Honey! I didn't mean that. I'm sorry Jane!"

Jane stood up, backing away from her mother. She seemed like a completely different person from what she had been ten minutes ago.

"Please, Jane, I didn't mean to!"

"That's no excuse! You hit me!"

"I'm sorry! It's a lot to process. Finding out about Will, about you knowing I haven't always been completely honest. I'm overwhelmed. I didn't mean to take my anger out on you."

"But you did."

"Jane, just listen, I would never do that. I would never hook up with someone without you knowing. Trust me, please."

"How can I when you've been lying to me for... how long?"

"I'll be better now. Please, Jane." Her mother's eyes begged, tears streaming down her face as she reached for Jane.

Jane couldn't be angry anymore. Her mom was right, it was a lot to take in. Jane's defensive mood started to shut down. Her mom looked broken, almost as if she was ready to give everything up.

Jane took her hand away from her face and touched her mother's arm. Instead of going to eat their very cold breakfast, they sat down on the couch. Jane grabbed her mother's hands with both of hers.

"I think we should call Will, Mom. May as well?"

Jane could tell her mother was nervous. She shook her head slightly, but she wasn't saying no. Her lips pressed into a thin line. Jane got up and grabbed her phone. She had a few notifications, but she ignored them. She sat back down next to her mom, still stiff with what had just happened.

Jane found Will's number and called him. She had no idea whether he would pick up or even if he would be awake. What was the time difference? Three rings and then it stopped. It took a moment to connect and then Jane heard his voice. Her mom let out a delighted shriek, startling both Jane and Will.

"Jane! Jane, are you ok? What's wrong?" Panic laced Will's groggy voice.

"I'm fine, it's ok. Sorry for waking you. That was mom."

Will fell silent in reply. The sound of his breath was soft, and Jane could practically hear his mind turning, trying to think of a reply.

Jane looked over to her mom. She held a cushion tight to her chest and covered her mouth with her hand. She was also speechless.

"Sorry. I know you told me not to, but she was singing Dad's favorite song this morning, and it just slipped when she started talking about you."

"Ah, shit, yeah that's ok Jane. Must've got the full blunt force of her wrath, huh?" He chuckled.

"Yeah, and more..." Jane laughed awkwardly. It felt so good to talk to him again. She grabbed her mom's hand and squeezed it, trying to transfer strength to her.

"Yeah, she's right here listening by the way."

Will's laugh turned nervous. "Mom? I'm sorry. Completely and utterly sorry. Hope you didn't tear into Jane too much."

Jane looked at her mom and passed the phone over. She cradled it in two hands, as if it were a newborn baby.

"Will?"

"Yes Mom, it's me."

"Oh my goodness, you're alive. I'm so, so sorry I pushed you away."

"I'm alive. Don't be sorry – I should be the one apologizing. I shouldn't have left; it was selfish of me, but I've sorted myself out now. I'm happy, and I'm so happy to be talking to you again."

"It's about time!" Jane nudged her mother and a laugh escaped her. All three of them chuckled.

"Yes, yes, I know. Anyway, I need to get back to sleep – big day here tomorrow. It was so good hearing your voice though. I'll call you and Jane again soon, I promise. I should be able to visit soon too."

"Oh ok, my love. Go back to bed."

"Love you, Mom."

"I love you too."

"Love you, Jane!" The line clicked as he hung up. Jane's mom held the phone close to her, not wanting to let it go.

"Did you hear that, Mom? He might be visiting us soon!" Jane said, ignoring the sting in her cheek.

Mom nodded, almost crying again. Jane could see she needed another hug, so she gave her a long hug and the phone finally released from her grasp.

"I'd better get myself sorted then!" Her mom stood up, brushed her hair to the side, and straightened her clothes. She walked off looking like she had a newfound purpose.

"Come on," she yelled back to Jane. "Let's have breakfast and then we are going to redecorate!"

Jane felt happiness radiate warmth through her. She couldn't help but forget about the slap, she loved her mom and knew she had done it out of shock. She knew what her mom meant by "redecorating" – she was going to put all the picture frames back up. Well, at least that's what Jane hoped.

*

It had been a long emotional day. The dusk shadows now spread throughout the sky. Jane's mom had to go to work again for another night shift – and she was actually going to work. Her mom had shown her proof that she was scheduled to work. Jane had asked for her to print out the rest of the month's schedule, so Jane wouldn't have to feel suspicious.

All day they had been looking through their boxed-up memories. They ended up placing pictures of each family member around the house. It started to feel like home again. Jane's mom even opened the door to Will's room. She couldn't quite bring herself to go in, but good things take time.

As Jane watched her reverse out of the driveway heading off to work, she still felt warm. She sat down at the kitchen benchtop, surrounded by her homework. She'd only poked at it throughout the day, but at least she still had Sunday to get it done.

She plugged her headphones into her phone and scrolled through her music. She needed some more upbeat songs on her playlist. Lately her taste had been pretty dreary.

A knock at the front door made her look up. She took her headphones out and walked over. She opened the door to find Theo's parents on the doorstep.

Theo's mom gave her a tense smile. "Hi, Jane. So rude of us to intrude on you, but can we talk?"

Jane blinked, shaking off her surprise. "Yes, sure." She moved to the side to let them in.

"Oh, don't worry we won't be long. Just don't want Theo to see." Theo's dad gave Jane a wink. He looked like a ghost, sinking in on himself.

They came inside and settled themselves on the couch. Jane perched on the edge of a chair. "What can I help you with?" she asked.

Theo's mom and dad looked at each other. "We know something happened between you two, and Theo's been quite down since then," his dad said.

"Oh, but we aren't here to talk about that," Sandra said quickly. "Everyone needs to move on, and we can't thank you enough for looking out for him the way you have."

"Would you like anything to drink?" Jane blurted out. She knew it wasn't an appropriate response, but she wanted to get as far away from the conversation as she could. Sandra opened her mouth to answer, but Jane bolted for the kitchen, before she could. She grabbed two glasses and filled them with water.

Footsteps followed and Jane turned to find them standing in the kitchen doorway. Jane held out the water and Sandra

stepped forward, taking the glasses, and brushing her hand against Jane's as she did. Her eyes were so sad.

"Look Jane, it's ok," Theo's dad said. "We just came to ask whether you could come over and help Theo. We heard… well, we think we know why you stopped walking with him."

Jane swallowed. She dropped her gaze, unable to meet their stares.

"Yes honey, people can be such bullies, but we believe you're still the same Jane that we met when you were a little kid."

"We were just wondering whether you could come over and get Theo back out in the garden. Ever since we told him about my cancer… well, that and whatever happened at school, he's been too upset to spend much time out there."

"And no pressure, you don't have to." Sandra squeezed Jane's hand. "You don't need to give us an answer right now, just pop over whenever you feel comfortable."

They sounded desperate. Jane finally found the strength to say something – to speak honestly.

"Yeah, I don't know. I'll think about it, if that's ok?" She already knew at some point she would pop over; she didn't have it in her heart not to.

Theo's parents looked disappointed, but nodded. His dad glanced down at Jane's homework. He pointed to an equation. "This one is 62." He looked back up at Jane and smiled. He turned away, walking toward the front door. Sandra started to follow, but stopped, turning around, and embracing Jane in a quick hug.

"Sorry, I'm a hugger." She snorted. "Love what you and your mom are doing with the place!"

She and Theo's dad walked out of the front door and back down the porch steps.

"See you soon!" Jane called after them. She thought that would give them a little glint of hope.

Jane closed the front door and walked back to her homework. She pressed play on the song she'd chosen earlier. She could feel this urge, like a gravitational pull, to go over there now, but she needed to think of an approach that wouldn't end in Theo yelling at her again.

She opened her messages, clicking on her mom's name.

COULD YOU PLEASE GET ANEMONE SEEDS FROM THE STORE WHEN YOU COME BACK TOMORROW MORNING? she wrote. She sent the message, then paused and added: IT'S FOR A PROJECT. LOVE YOU X

That was only a little lie after all.

15.


Jane


Walking down the steps the next morning, Jane felt anxious. Her homework still sat on the benchtop where she'd left it, but on top of that was a note from her mom and a pack of anemone seeds. Next to it, her mom had placed one of her favorite snacks.

Jane picked up the note. She wasn't surprised when she read that her mom would be asleep for most of the day, but she promised to make a lasagna for dinner. Her mom had also written that she wanted them to have a good catch-up that evening, and maybe even ring Will too.

Jane popped some bread in the toaster. She glanced over her homework while she waited for the toast to finish, but the numbers seemed to rearrange themselves before her eyes.

She would go over to Theo's soon, so she could get him off her mind. Quickly eating her breakfast, she ran upstairs. She paused for a second, looking into her brother's room before continuing to her own. She chucked on a pair of corduroy dungarees with a long-sleeve tee underneath. She brushed her hair, leaving it down, and put on some lip gloss.

She grabbed her air force ones and ran back downstairs. This was it, she thought, time to make peace. She grabbed the seeds off the counter and put on a coat. She swung open the door with a newfound determination.

It felt like it took years to reach Theo's front door, her anxiety growing with each step. She knocked lightly at first and waited. Maybe she was too early? She looked behind her, secretly scared of someone from school spotting her.

The door opened. It was Theo's dad, Troy. His smile almost melted her heart. Tears welled in his eyes, and he pulled her into a hug. Jane felt awkward with the sudden emotional response but relaxed in his grasp. It was nice to be hugging a dad even if it wasn't hers.

Letting go, he closed the door behind her. "Go on out to the garden, love. I'll get Theo." He made his way upstairs, taking a breather in between each step. Jane watched him disappear and then set off towards the garden. She sat down on the little garden bench and waited, nerves flying around in her stomach.

Twenty minutes later, she was still waiting. Her nerves were bubbling over, almost persuading her to give up and run.

She could hear voices upstairs, probably Theo refusing to come out. Then it sounded like someone was having a shower. Awkwardly, Jane got up and wandered around the garden. It made her sad to see it in this condition. Whenever she'd looked out her window, it had always looked so glorious. Now, it looked like it was dying. Even taking into account the shift to winter, his garden shouldn't have been this bare.

Her thoughts spiraled off. Maybe this was how Theo felt right now – the dying plants a mirror of his depression.

The door opened behind her. She froze. Footsteps approached and then walked around her. Jane looked at his shoes. She didn't know what to do; she hadn't thought that far ahead.

She fiddled with the seed packet and accidentally ripped it. The seeds dispersed everywhere. She heard herself gasp and knelt down, trying to gather them. She heard Theo murmur something, then he knelt next to her, helping. She still hadn't looked at him yet. His hand brushed hers and a tingle rushed up her arm. Unable to help herself, she glanced up. He stared back at her.

"Hey."

"Hi," she replied, blushing. They stood, and he passed her some more seeds.

"I thought you might want these to plant. Sorry I spilled them." She pushed the packet toward him. He cupped them in his hands delicately. A slow smile spread across his face as he read the label, sending warmth throughout Jane's body.

"Let's go sit down." He turned and walked to the bench.

Jane followed a few steps behind. She watched him take careful steps around his muddy garden. She hadn't noticed how much it had been raining lately.

Theo took a big step over a patch of mud. She thought she would go around it, since her legs weren't that long. She regretted her decision immediately. Her foot slipped from underneath her. She tried to stop herself from falling, but landed in the mud. A squeal escaped her lips before she hit the ground and the wind was knocked out of her. Now looking up at the moody sky, she felt the wetness seep through her clothes.

"Are you ok? Jane?!" Theo yelled.

There was no air in Jane's chest to reply. She raised her arm with a thumbs up instead. She should have predicted her clumsiness would get in the way.

Raising her head, she looked up at Theo. He reached out a hand to pull her up. She took it, but at the last minute, gave it a yank pulling him down into the mud with her. She started to laugh and heard Theo join her. He rolled onto his side, swiveling around to lie next to her. She couldn't stop laughing. He grinned at her, the smile spreading across his face.

She reached for him but her hand froze in mid-air. The memory of his crushed expression flashed in her mind, and she drew back. She had hurt him. She'd forgotten about it all for a split second. Immediately her laughter stopped, and a frown creased her forehead.

"I'm sorry," she said.

"I know you are." Theo held her gaze and silence fell over them. Jane tried to find her words, but he spoke again. "A lot of things have changed. And I've finally realized that that's ok. And I'm ok with you ditching me now… but I still miss hanging out with you."

Jane let out a breath. She had never expected him to tell her how he really felt.

"Yeah, I miss hanging out with you too."

"Is that why you came over?"

Jane almost replied with a "yes", but it would be better if she was honest, considering she was trying to rekindle their friendship.

"No. Well, yes and no. Your parents asked me to come over. They were concerned about you."

Theo frowned, his face starting to close off.

"But that wasn't the only reason I came over," Jane said quickly. "You left me a flower, and I wanted to come and say thank you too. So… thank you."

"How'd you know it was me?"

"Who else would give me a flower?"

"I don't know." Theo grinned. "The boogie man?"

"The boogie man?" Jane cracked up laughing again and Theo joined her. She gave him a little shove. He grabbed her hand and pulled her closer to him.

"I did miss you too though," Jane said quietly.

"Knew it." Theo hesitated. "Can I ask you something?"

"Sure, anything." Anxiety started to crawl through Jane.

Theo didn't meet her eyes this time. "Why did you stop hanging out with me?"

Jane let the silence hang for a moment. "It felt so good to be a part of something." The words felt thick in her mouth and they came out quiet. "I didn't want to be seen as the freak's friend anymore. That's my honest answer."

Theo cleared his throat, "…thanks."

"And even though we are hanging now, I still want to tell you that it may not be the same at school. I'll try to put more effort into saying hi between classes, but… I just, I don't know Theo. I don't want to be called that again."

"That's fair enough," Theo said. His voice low, but he didn't sound too upset. "But I'm not really a freak anyway."

"Theo…" Jane swore her heart broke a little hearing him say that. "You were never a freak."

He raised his head and looked down at Jane. She felt like she had been as honest as she could, and she hoped it hadn't

hurt him. It must be so hard to have judgments made about you all the time, just for being a little different.

"What are we going to do Jane?"

Jane frowned. "What do you mean?"

"With this garden?" He raised his hands in an all-encompassing gesture. "With everything?"

Jane reached out, squeezing his arm. "Start again perhaps?"

"Sounds good to me."

*

Jane and Theo lay in the mud together for the next half an hour, brainstorming ideas. Theo did most of the brainstorming. Jane liked listening to him talk about things he was passionate about. She put in an idea every now and again. She wanted to put a hammock in an overgrown part of the garden.

Surprisingly, Theo liked the idea of having an overgrown part in the garden. Usually, he wanted his garden to be straight, nice and tidy, but he said letting some of it be "free" made him feel free in a way too.

He frowned, considering his own words. "That doesn't make sense," he said.

Jane shook her head. "No, it does. It's like… less restrained. Nothing to hold it – or you – back."

Theo nodded slowly. "I like that."

The sky then opened up on the two of them. Jane started to hop up, but Theo pulled her back down. They both couldn't stop giggling. They opened their arms wide and embraced the rain. After a while, they both got up, again laughing at the sight of each other.

They got to work, ripping out the weeds and plants Theo no longer wanted. The time passed quickly, laughing and chatting in amongst the work.

Finally, Jane told Theo she had homework to do back at home, but she would be over tomorrow afternoon. She didn't want to leave, but she couldn't fall behind in school. Before turning around and going through their connecting backyard gate, she gave him a quick hug.

Once in her own yard, she kicked off her muddy shoes outside her back door, not wanting to bring any mud inside, then ran upstairs and got into the shower.

Throwing on some comfy clothes, she grabbed her phone, then headed back downstairs. She only cared about one notification, a message from Theo: I NEEDED THAT.

Warmth spread throughout her again before she replied: SAME.

16.

Jane

Jane couldn't keep up. Days passed every time she blinked. It had gotten much colder as fall turned to winter. With trying to steer clear of Jack, hanging out with Theo a bit more, and reconnecting with her mom, life had been a lot for her recently. She felt overwhelmed but she also felt so, so happy. Will was even organizing a visit!

She loved going over to Theo's place to help him with his garden and just hanging out with him in general. Despite the other stresses, it made her feel peaceful.

Even though it was winter, they still mucked around in the garden. Sometimes they didn't do any work, they simply talked. She loved how passionate he was about his interests. She wished she was strong enough to stand up to the bullies at school, not only for herself but for him too.

Even without Jack, school wasn't going smoothly. Exams had crept closer, and Jane had been called out by her teacher a few times. She remembered the students around her snickering as her teacher rambled on about how important these exams were, and told her she would have to get a move on if she wanted to pass. She realized she would have to get her priorities straight even if that meant not hanging with Theo as often.

Today, school dragged. Thursday the 5th of December – she had a week before her practice tests started. The real tests were closer to the summer break, but the mock exams were just as important. If she could just get through them, she could relax over the Christmas and New Year break.

She hated how close the practice tests were to Christmas. Christmas was all about sharing happiness around, but it was hard to do that when you were stressed about failing.

She walked through her backyard over to Theo's house, passing her mom who was grabbing some decorations out of the shed. Will was hopefully going to be here for the holidays

113

and her mother couldn't be more excited. It made her smile to see her mom this happy again.

Theo was waiting for her on his bench. She sat down next to him, feeling awkward with what she was about to tell him.

He glanced at her, tensing up as he took in her body language.

"I have to tell you something," Jane said.

"I can tell."

"I got called out in class today. I'm letting my grades slip and I didn't even realize exams are only a week away!"

Theo frowned. "Ok… and what's that got to do with me?"

Jane sighed. "I've just been so distracted lately and I just need everything to go back to normal for a while."

"So… like how it was? When you ignored me?"

"No! Well, kind of… I don't know, Theo. It's so hard, ok?"

"Don't be ridiculous."

"Look, I'm not going to ignore you, Theo. I just can't hang out as much anymore. I need to put school first for a while."

"Mhmm." He stood up from the bench and started walking towards his back door.

Jane ran after him, catching his hand. "Please don't be mad, I don't know what else to do. I really need to study."

He looked at her with such disappointment, Jane had to drop her gaze.

He sighed and turned back to her. "Ok. Just don't leave, leave me."

"I won't. I'll text you!" Jane said.

He squeezed her hand, then let go and walked through his back door. Jane smiled to herself. That didn't go as bad as she'd thought.

*

Theo

Theo had known Jane would back away at some point. He didn't know why he'd had his hopes up so much thinking this

time would be different. They had been hanging out for almost two full months though, so he tried not to let it upset him.

Theo could tell Jane felt bad, but still, if only she just dropped her friend group and status at school and learned not to care, nothing would have to change. Oh well. Theo didn't want to be one of the reasons she flunked school, so he would just let her be for a while.

It hurt him walking away from her. She looked like a lost puppy, but what else was he supposed to do?

Going to school the next two weeks had a different feeling to it. Theo saw Jane now and again, but she was always rushing somewhere. She was either heading off to her next class, sitting a practice test, or studying somewhere. She didn't even pay attention to her "friends". She really was focusing on school which made Theo feel a bit better. He did secretly look forward to the nights though – that's when Jane would come online, and they would chat about anything and everything for hours. It seemed easier to tell her how he felt over messages, but he did miss her physical presence.

It was the last day of school – the last day of practice tests before their small winter break. Theo woke that morning, disoriented. He wasn't quite sure where he was. After a few seconds of staring into space, it all clicked. He remembered his mom had knocked on his door waking him, but he'd drifted back to sleep.

He checked his phone – one unread message from Jane. He went to reply but then noticed the time – 8:50 a.m. He'd never jumped out of bed so fast!

He fumbled around, finding something to throw on, then grabbed some shoes and his backpack and sprinted downstairs. He took the stairs three at a time, running into the kitchen when he reached the bottom.

He found his mom and gave her a quick kiss on the cheek. She handed him an apple and he ran out the front door, not even closing it behind him. He had his final exam at 9:15 a.m., and he was supposed to arrive ten minutes early. He didn't even stop to look when crossing the road. All he could think about was that he couldn't be late for his last exam.

He entered the school grounds but didn't slow his pace. He ran past Nico who gave him a wave which Theo returned. He even ran past Jack, actually making Jack jump in fright. He would have savored that moment if he'd had time. Jack was also late for the exam. He reached his English class and swung the door open, the posters on the walls wriggled in place, from the wind the door had created. Everyone in the class jumped, startled.

"Look who finally decided to turn up! Theodore Williams, you're late." The teacher growled.

"I know. I'm sorry, Sir. I overslept. I'm so sorry."

"This is your last year of school, Theo. You need to take this more seriously."

"I know, I really didn't mean to. Again, I am sorry."

"Just don't be late again. Go take a seat."

"Yes, thanks, ok. Sorry again, Sir." Theo walked down the aisle, gazing at the rest of the students. He noticed Jack had slipped in quietly while he was getting told off. He threw Theo a smirk. He could feel the heat of Mr Thompson's eyes on his back.

Theo spotted Jane nervously glancing at him, but he gave her a quick thumbs up which seemed to make her less tense.

Theo found a seat and sat down.

*

Three hours later, Theo put down his pen. That was the longest and hardest practice test he had ever sat. He'd still been writing, right up until the last moment they were allowed. Most of the other students had left – Theo suspected they'd given up because it was so hard. However, there were a handful of other kids still writing away when the alarm went off. Jane was one of them. They handed their papers forward and started to pack their bags.

"Was I the only one that thought that was hard, or did you think it was as well?" Jane asked him.

"Yeah, it was hard."

"Like impossible hard! Ughh." She seemed frustrated and Theo didn't really know what to do about that. He decided to put his arm around her shoulders and give her a light squeeze. She didn't move away which was a good sign.

"At least we're free for a while now," he said, hoping to make her feel better.

She just nodded, and they walked out of class together. Once out of class, she seemed to distance herself from him, but he wasn't surprised.

"So, what are your plans now?" she asked awkwardly.

"I think I might just go home, but first I need to check if I have to finish anything else on my art assignment."

"…do you want any help?"

This made him smile. "Sure." They headed down the hall to his art class.

When they reached the art room, he felt as though she was tugged back. Maybe she was overthinking… being cautious about being seen with him. He continued in, unsure what to do about that. The sun came through the wall of windows, warming Theo. He then looked around at the new paintings hanging up across the classroom before seeing Poppy.

She must've been finishing up her assignment. Was that why Jane hadn't come in? Theo couldn't believe he'd started to think Jane didn't care as much about her image anymore.

He turned around, expecting Jane to be just behind him, but she wasn't there. Annoyance overran him. He walked back out of the class into the hall.

A yelp rang out, and he stopped dead. Down the end of the hallway, he saw Jane, a boy's arm around her waist, his hand over her mouth.

"Jane!"

Who was that?! Theo raced down the hallway towards her, but the boy pulled her around the corner.

"Jane! Leave her alone."

Theo ran around the corner, but he could only see Tommy, one of Jack's hounds, no sign of Jane. Tommy opened a locker door, pretending to be interested in the contents. Pathetic.

Theo strode towards him. "Where is she?"

Tommy turned to him, a stupid grin on his face. "What do you mean, dude?"

"I am not your 'dude'. Where's Jane?" He pushed Tommy back, angrily.

"Whoa, whoa, you really want to do this?"

"Don't be a dick, Tommy." Poppy jogged up the corridor towards them. "Where's Jane?"

"Just stay out of this, Poppy," Tommy barked back.

But Poppy pushed in between him and Theo. "Are you serious? What's going on? Theo, what did you see?"

Theo blinked; surprised Poppy even knew his name. She didn't even call him "Freak".

"Someone grabbed Jane. I think he was hurting her," he told her.

Poppy turned back to Tommy. "I'm going to scream if you don't tell me."

"No, you won't."

Theo felt like he was watching six-year-olds argue over a toy.

"Yes, I will. Three… two…" Poppy took a big mouthful of air and Theo got ready to cover his ears.

Tommy clapped his hand over her mouth. "Ok, ok, just chill. Jane's outside, talking to Jack."

"What the heck, dude?" Nico's voice rang out. "Get your hands off her!"

Theo, Poppy, and Tommy all turned at once, startled. Nico reached them. He pushed Tommy back.

Tommy grabbed him. Poppy got between them, and Nico yelled again. He shoved Tommy away. The three of them stumbled back, falling over in a big mess.

Theo stepped towards them, but Poppy waved him away. "Go help Jane," she yelled.

Theo ran down the hall and outside. He should have asked Tommy where outside, he realized, but he wouldn't have been surprised if he didn't know.

"Jane!" he yelled. He heard a thud and some scuffling, but he couldn't tell where from. Theo broke into a sprint.

## 17

Jane

Jack grabbed Jane by the wrist after Tommy handed her off to him. She stumbled after him. He had a steel grip, and she couldn't wriggle her hand out of it.

Jack pulled her outside and behind the gymnasium, dragging her into the small corner. He came to a stop and let go of her hand.

Jane looked around. They were sheltered from all students' and teachers' gazes. She was cornered, literally. No one would see what was about to happen, her chances of getting help were slimming with every second that passed.

Jane rubbed her wrist, glaring at Jack. He shoved her, suddenly. She fell over, hard, the gravel cutting into her palms as she landed.

"What was that for?" she yelled.

"Oh come on, don't be so stupid, Jane." Jack crouched over her, making her shrink away. "You and your little freak seem to be getting closer, huh? What did I tell you?"

Jane stared at him. "You can't control me," she said firmly. She tried to get up, but he shoved her back.

"Oh honey," he whispered. "I already do."

Shivers ran through Jane, the temperature seeming to drop a few degrees. Jack let go, and Jane stood, brushing off all the grit. He watched her, his face impassive. Jane eyed him, then tried to walk past. He stepped in front of her, blocking her way. Jane's heart hammered in her chest. She stepped to the left, and he blocked her path again.

"Don't be a dick!"

"Don't be a dick, huh?" Jack's voice was scarily calm, then anger seemed to explode out of him. He threw himself at Jane, smashing both of them against the wall. "Don't be a dick? You're the one who's being a dick, Jane. You haven't been paying attention at all to anything lately. Do you even

know about the party tonight, huh? Or are you ignoring that too?"

Jane shook her head. She couldn't believe it. All this was over a party? She had seen messages on the group chat, choosing to ignore them. She had already decided she wasn't going. This was insane.

"I don't want to go, Jack." She pushed him back, instantly regretting it.

He grabbed her face, pulling her close. "Too bad, princess. Also, this crap with The Freak has to stop."

"What crap? And you must be deaf, because I remember telling you his name is Theo."

A small part of Jane told her she was in dangerous territory, but she didn't care anymore. How much worse could things get? He had already gotten her cornered and pushed up against a wall.

Jack shook his head, slowly. "You really don't care, do you?"

"Jane!"

Jane's head whipped around at Theo's shout. Panic flashed across Jack's face, and a surge of adrenaline coursed through Jane. She raised her knee, hitting Jack right where the sun doesn't shine. She took off running around the gym toward Theo's voice.

"Theo!" she yelled, but Jack was right behind her.

Jack grabbed her, hauling her backward. They fell, both of them slamming into the ground. Somehow, Jane landed on top, but he quickly overturned them, holding her arms down.

Jane tried to scream, but he shoved his hand over her mouth, muffling the sound.

Jane thrashed. She tried to wriggle out from under him, but there was no use. She gasped for breath, his weight pressing on her chest. Everything went black around the edges.

"Wrong move," Jack hissed. "You'll regret that."

"Get off me!" Jane screamed into his hand.

"You're mine, and I'm going to prove it at the party tonight. You can't escape me that easily."

"You're a psycho!" Jane heard footsteps not far away. "Theo!" she yelled again. The footsteps came to an abrupt stop.

Hot pain raced through Jane's cheek, a familiar feeling. Her head twisted suddenly as the slap echoed in her ear. She still couldn't breathe.

"Jane!"

Jane heard Theo's shout, but everything went fuzzy. The weight of Jack lifted off her, and she tried to regain her bearings. Scuffling came from her left, and she scrambled back trying to get out of the way.

Her vision finally cleared. Theo slammed into Jack. Jane stood and quickly regretted it. She fell back, still dizzy.

Theo tried to move towards her, reaching for her hand. Jack pulled him back, throwing him to the ground.

Jack looked back at Jane, his eyes wild. One of them was swelling, Theo's punch taking effect. This gave her strength. Jane went to stand again. Theo moved to help, but Jack shoved him.

Jane used the wall as support. Jack and Theo both watched her rise.

"Enough, Jack. Move." Jane poured every ounce of strength she had left into keeping her voice steady.

Jack started to laugh.

"Do what she says man," Theo said, his tone dark. "Move."

"I like how you think it's that easy. Look at yourselves."

"Move," Theo and Jane said, almost in unison.

"Uh-uh-uh, use your manners." Jack grinned, taking pleasure in this new game.

Jane almost gave in, ready to plead and beg, when Theo shot her a look that could kill. Without even meaning to, Jane was playing into the game.

Jack's cackling stopped. "Oh. Ok then." He lunged towards Theo.

His fist made contact with Theo's jaw, knocking him down with one punch. Neither of them saw it coming. Theo hit the ground hard, blood splattering out of his mouth. He groaned

and tried to push himself up. Jack's foot slammed into his ribs.

Air rushed out of Theo. He gasped, all of his strength focused on getting his breath back.

"No!" Jane sidestepped Jack, racing to Theo's side. She blocked another blow from Jack.

Jack froze, stopping himself before hitting her.

Jane grabbed Theo's face. "Breathe! Just breathe."

Theo's eyes were wide, and Jane could read the pain in his face. Blood dribbled from the corner of his mouth. He let out a shaky breath, then sucked in another one. He grabbed Jane's hand, squeezing it tight. He pulled her closer, whispering, "Run".

Jane shook her head. She couldn't leave him.

"Right, that's enough." Jack grabbed Jane's shoulders trying to pry her away.

Panic rose through Jane, and Theo gripped her hand tighter.

"You're coming whether you want to or not. Don't make things difficult."

Jack grabbed her, prying Theo's fingers back. Pain flashed across Theo's face and Jane's grip loosened. She couldn't watch him in pain; he couldn't get hurt anymore because of her. Fear overtook his expression, as if he read her mind.

"Jane, don't!"

Jane let go.

Jack dragged her back, now turning both of them away from the gym and on to the field. Theo screamed her name. She turned around and kicked at Jack's grasp. He let go for a second before grabbing a bunch of her hair, jerking her back.

This time, it was Jane's turn to scream. Jack muffled the sound with his other hand.

Jane looked desperately back towards Theo. He'd stopped moving. Her eyes strained to see whether he was breathing. She didn't know if she was imagining it, but she thought she saw his chest rise.

He had to be. He couldn't be dead.

Jack stopped and faced her. He shook her, hard.

"Jane... Jane! Stop struggling. If you had just listened, this never would have happened!"

"If YOU listened, this would have never happened!" she screamed.

"Just SHUT UP!" he yelled back, raising his hand and hitting the side of her head.

Light evaporated. Jane's whole body relaxed suddenly. She felt him pick her up and toss her over his shoulder like a sack of potatoes. With each knock her head took, as she swung back and forth, the more she invited the silence in.

18.

Theo

Theo awoke to darkness.

"Jane? Are you there? Please be here…" He whimpered. He reached out, hoping to feel Jane next to him. Instead, his hand met a layer of frost surrounding him. How long had he been lying in the gravel? How long had Jane been gone?

He pushed himself up, taking it slowly. Worry prickled through him. He had to find her. The pressure in his head built, the further upright he got. He gazed around, eyes straining in the dim moonlight. No sign of Jane; no sign of anyone.

He wasn't surprised that no one had found him. The gymnasium loomed over him, hiding him from sight.

He felt in his pocket. Thankfully, his phone hadn't been damaged in the fight, but the sudden brightness made him recoil in pain. He squinted, as his eyes adjusted to the light. It read 9:12 p.m.

He unlocked the screen, panic rising as he scrolled through the endless list of messages from his parents. Not one message was from Jane.

A message from an unknown number topped the list. He swiped it open.

YO ARE YOU ALRIGHT? CAN'T FIND YOU ANYWHERE. NICO.

Theo went to reply, but his phone started ringing. It was his mom. Sighing, he picked up.

"THEO? Theo, is that you? Where are you?"

"Yes, Mom, it's me."

"Where have you been? Why haven't you been answering your—"

"Mom, Mom! It's ok. I'm coming home now. I was just hanging out with some friends, and my phone was on silent." He lied. His phone volume was up loud. He wouldn't be surprised if she replied saying that he had no friends.

125

"For goodness' sake, you could've at least messaged me. You had us both worried sick!"

"I know, I'm sorry. I'll see you soon." Theo hung up before she could reply. Her voice hadn't made him feel any better. He moved back toward the wall and held onto it, needing the support.

He put his hand up to his face. He felt dried blood on his cheek. He followed it up finding a bigger cut, sticky with congealed blood. His eye was all puffy and he winced when he touched it.

Leaning heavily against the wall, he made his way slowly around the gym, hoping to find his bag somewhere. He found it near the hall exit, tossed to the side. He didn't remember throwing it.

He picked it up and pulled out his jacket. The chill from the frost had finally kicked in. He felt himself shaking, the cold attacking his insides. He picked up his pace – or he tried to anyway – and started making his way home, the light from the moon guiding him.

Another ping sounded from his phone. He fumbled to grab it, hoping it would be Jane. But it was just Nico again.

C'MON, YOU ALIVE?

Theo took a quick selfie, the light blinding him, and sent that to Nico, mostly to show Nico what his "friend" had done to his face. A few seconds later his phone rang.

Theo answered it, and Nico launched in with a hundred questions. Loud music and laughter surrounded his voice, and Theo's head pounded. The words all melded together.

"Stop, Nico, just stop!"

"Shit, sorry dude."

Theo heard a door close, and the background noise dropped away.

"But your face…" Nico said, quieter now. "Are you ok? Seriously?"

"No… I mean, I'd be ok if I knew where Jane was."

There was a long pause, then Nico cleared his throat. "I know where she is." Shame laced Nico's voice.

"What? Where?" Theo said, his heart pounding.

"She's here, at this party."

"Are you serious?"

"Yeah. I didn't see her come in, but she just walked downstairs with Poppy a couple of minutes ago."

"I thought…" Theo replayed the scene in his mind. Jack had dragged Jane away. He'd hurt her, and then taken her away, leaving Theo on the ground. "Did Jack take her there?"

"Looks like it, but I dunno. Sorry, I couldn't help you. Tommy grabbed Poppy, and I couldn't leave her."

"It's ok, I understand."

But Theo didn't really understand – he couldn't understand any of what had happened today. Theo heard music in the background again, and his head throbbed.

"I shouldn't tell you this…" Nico hesitated, then continued in a rush. "But Jack has really started to piss me off lately. I like you dude; I wanna hang out with you more than him. Thing is, Jack sent me a picture about ten minutes ago on our group chat and—"

"What is it? Get to the point." Theo's impatience rose.

"Yeah, ok, look I'll just send it to you. Before you say anything, I don't think it's real. Like, look at her face… I just thought you should know since you two are close. Maybe you can help her? I don't know."

Theo swallowed, a feeling of dread rising inside him. "Just send it, Nico."

"Ok, ok, I need to go in a sec, but we should go for a run together, yeah? So… you know, so we can chat or something?" Nico sounded like he was still hiding something, but Theo shook the feeling off.

"Yeah, sure, sure. Message me. And thanks."

Theo hung up the phone. He stared at it, impatiently waiting for the photo. What had Nico so nervous? Theo's imagination went wild with worst-case scenarios.

An eternity later, a message came through. It was a screenshot of the group chat. Jack had sent a photo – Jane laying asleep on his chest. Underneath it, a message read "MINE" with a little lock emoji.

Rage swelled inside Theo. He was about to throw his phone at the pavement, when Nico messaged again.

ZOOM IN, LOOK CLOSER.

Theo took a deep breath, swallowing down his rising emotions. He went back to the screenshot and zoomed in on Jane's face. Looking closer, he could just make out the bruising on her forehead, near her hairline. He could also see slight color differences up her arms. Theo zoomed in on Jack's face which, with the help of the filter he'd put over the photo, showed just a slight yellow stain around his eye and a little split on his lip. This was taken today, after the fight.

Jane's face was slack, she wasn't asleep but unconscious. Whenever he took this photo, Jane was most likely not even aware. Rage rushed through Theo again as he called Nico back.

"Theo?"

"What the heck, dude?"

"I know it's so wrong, I'm sorry I couldn't have helped you out..." Nico sounded guilty.

"Where are you?"

"At Brittany's house... dude. You're not thinking about coming over here, are you?"

"Why else do you think I asked?! Of course I am!"

"Nooo, no! You can't!"

"Why?" Theo yelled.

"You will literally get pummelled to the ground. I'm not joking. You won't leave alive. Everyone will back Jack up."

"Even you?"

"Whoa. Dude. I never said I would. What he did was seriously wrong. Just, I don't want things to get any worse, ok? I'll make sure either Poppy or I are always next to her. Poppy went to find her as soon as the message came through."

"I should call the police."

"NO, DON'T!"

Silence followed Nico's shout. Dread built inside Theo again. "What aren't you telling me? I know you are hiding something else. Please tell me." Theo's voice caught at the end of his sentence. More silence on Nico's end. "Nico, please…"

"Ok, ok… Jack sent me another photo. I'm not sure he sent it to anyone else. Maybe he knew I would call you, so that's why he sent it to me? As like a threat perhaps…"

"Nico, seriously, move on."

"It's a revealing photo, dude." His voice sounded like a whisper. "Of just her…"

Another wave of rage crashed through Theo and this time he couldn't stop it. Without realizing what he was doing, he grabbed his bag off his back and threw it at the ground.

*

It took Theo more than half an hour to limp the short distance home. He felt disorientated, sure he'd taken a few wrong turns.

Light spilled from the front of Jane's house. Theo stumbled up the porch steps and knocked on her door. Footsteps came from inside. Maybe she was already home.

Theo closed his eyes. She was here. Jane was ok now. Or mostly ok. He wondered if she knew about the photos.

To his surprise, a stranger opened the door, he looked familiar.

"Hi?"

"Who are you?" Theo knew his words were blunt, but he didn't care right now.

The familiar looking stranger in front of him frowned, then his expression changed as he took in the blood and injuries covering Theo's face. "My name's Will," he said. "What happened to your face? Did someone hurt you?" Will glanced behind Theo, as if he was looking for the attacker.

Theo couldn't help but look, flinching, even though nothing was behind him. An urge to rock tugged at him but he resisted it. He turned back to Will who looked just about ready to close the door on him.

"Is she here? Jane, I mean? I… have I got the wrong house?"

Will laughed, though it had a nervous quality to it. "Jane's not here. I don't know where she is. You have the right house. I'm her brother."

"Ohhhh. Ok, thanks." Theo turned to walk down the porch steps finally realizing why Will seemed familiar.  Will followed him down the steps.

"Do you know where Jane is? Is she in trouble?" Will's gaze traveled over the cut on Theo's face again.

Theo thought about telling him the truth, but a different truth came out.

"I think she's at an end-of-practice-tests party." Theo walked down the steps then looked back at Will. "I'm Theo," he said. "Jane's friend. I'm a neighbor too." Theo felt like utter shit not telling the truth, but he guessed if he told him, Will would've insisted on calling the police.

Theo walked over to his house. For some reason, he felt obliged to knock on his front door once he was in front of it instead of opening it himself. It swung open, and his teary-eyed mother stared out at him. Theo looked down at her, not even attempting to hide his face. She gasped and covered her mouth. His dad appeared in the doorway beside her. Instead of staring, he grabbed Theo by the shoulder and brought him inside.

They stood in the entranceway, none of them saying anything. Theo's dad was the first to move. He disappeared into the kitchen and brought back an ice pack wrapped in a dish towel. He handed it to Theo and he put it on his eye, suddenly realizing how much it had been throbbing. The ice burned at first, then the heat in his face diminished, taking some of the pain with it.

"So, are you going to tell us what happened?" his dad asked, "Or are we all going to ignore this until the morning?"

Theo looked to and fro between his parents. Their expressions flitted between anger and concern as they waited for him to reply. Theo had to tell them something now, he realized.

"Look, I was leaving school when I accidentally knocked into someone and they hit me back. But it's fine; I'm fine now. I don't want to tell anyone about this. Then I needed to blow off steam, so Nico and I ran around the track for a while. Ok?"

His mom shook her head. "You expect us to believe that?"

"Well… yeah?"

"Alright, fine. Whatever happened, we're just glad you're home now." Theo's dad patted him on the back.

Theo gave a small grimace. "I need to sleep," he said, and headed upstairs.

He closed his door behind him, then slid a chair underneath the handle. His parents had banned locks as when he was younger Theo had barricaded himself in the bathroom during a meltdown.

He let his bag slip to the ground.

He stared across to Jane's window, hoping to see Jane inside. He wasn't surprised when all he saw was her anemone dying on the windowsill, they only lasted four to eight days in a vase.

Theo fell back onto his bed, clenching his fists and punching them into either side of his mattress. He stifled a rage-filled yell. He sat up out of breath. He was so angry, his temper boiled. He felt useless. He hadn't saved Jane and he couldn't do anything until Jane was home. It wasn't fair. Theo reached over to his bedside lamp, picked it up, and threw it across the room.

19.


Jane


Waking up in Jack's arms was a fear that Jane never knew existed. Her eyes snapped open and she bolted upright, startling him. He jumped, arm flying from her shoulder and Jane scrambled off the bed to the other side of the room. She pressed herself into the wall, trying to get as far away from him as possible.

He chuckled, slowly getting up from the bed and strolling over. Jane dived for the door, but suddenly he was in front of her. Jane pushed back into the wall, trying to disappear. Jack moved in close, invading her bubble. He cupped her jaw, turning her face to the side and whispering in her ear.

"I told you. You're mine. Don't make me prove it again."

Then he kissed her on the ear. His finger drifted down to her neckline, flicking her shirt buttons to the side.

Her buttons were open.

Jane cowered. Fear took over her, dreading what he would do next.

"If you tell anyone what happened tonight, you're done for. Got it?"

Jane didn't want to nod; she didn't want to look at him. She wanted him as far away from her as possible.

"Look at me!" Jack's hand snapped back to her jaw, twisting her head back toward him. "Open your eyes, Jane."

Jane opened them slowly. His phone was in front of her face. At the bottom of his camera roll were two rows of skin-colored photos. She peered closer and cautiously tapped a photo. She couldn't believe what she was staring at, a sense of familiarity took over. It was her.

Her heartbeat quickened. She flicked to the next photo, revealing her face next to her exposed skin. She wanted to throw up. He was a monster.

"What the heck?" A whisper came out of her.

Jack took the phone away from her face. She reached out to grab it back, grabbing air instead. Jack pushed her back into the wall, his hand firm on her shoulder.

"You go to the police… you tell anyone, and everyone – and I mean everyone – will see what a whore you actually are. Gosh, actually sending me photos Jane! Who would've guessed you wanted me that badly?" A sarcastic smile crossed Jack's face. "See you down at the party." His last sentence was more of a command then a question.

Jane closed her eyes. He was going to end her. She wished for it to be over. His hand disappeared from her shoulder. She slid to the floor. She heard him step back and open the door. She risked peeking out. Jack was gone, leaving her alone in the room.

As simple as that, she felt destroyed once again. She stared at the gaping doorway. Music came from that direction. He'd taken her to the party. She'd been unconscious, and he'd dragged her there! He had done more than drag her there. She felt completely exposed as she rushed to do up her buttons.

Of course, he brought her to the party. How else could he prove that he had "won"? She wanted to get out there as soon as possible but if she did, would that make him leak the photos?

Shit! Theo! Jane scrambled through her pockets, but found nothing – no phone, no wallet, nothing!

She quickly stood and looked around the room for her bag, but it was nowhere to be seen. It was probably back at school, just like Theo, lying outside in the cold, unconscious.

A clock on the wall read 9 p.m. Jane rubbed her eyes, trying to think of a way out of her situation. She didn't even know whose house she was at – whose party had it been?

Someone dashed past the doorway and Jane cringed. Was it Jack coming back? She heard her name being called, a familiar safe voice, and wondered if she was imagining it. But then the figure came back, stopping and turning in the doorway.

"Poppy," she whispered, her voice cracking.

"Jane! Oh, thank god. Are you… oh shit, look at your face!" Poppy crossed the room in a few steps, pulling Jane into a hug. They sat down on the edge of the bed. It was the last place Jane wanted to be after waking up there, but she didn't have the strength to move.

Poppy's arms were lined with bruises too. "What happened to you?" Jane asked, touching Poppy's arm gently.

Poppy shook her head. "Tommy started picking on Theo and I was trying to get him to stop, but that ended up in Nico and Tommy fighting because he pushed me yada, yada, yada… But I can't complain. Are you alright? Where's Theo?"

Jane clasped her hands together and looked down at them. The sudden realization of what had just happened hit her. Adrenaline had been covering up her pain, until then.

"I… um, yeah… I don't know. He got us both pretty good, I think? All I can remember is being dragged away from Theo." Tears brimmed at the edge of Jane's eyes, and she rubbed them away. "Theo wasn't moving. I don't know if he's…"

Poppy said nothing. She instead held out her hand and stood, leading Jane to the bathroom. Poppy locked the door behind them and switched on the light. Jane almost didn't recognize the girl staring back at her in the mirror.

"This is not ok Jane. We need to tell someone."

"No. No!" Terror filled Jane at the idea as she remembered Jack's threat. He would ruin her – ruin all her chances of getting into a good college, getting a job, getting anything. "Poppy we can't! It'll just get worse. If anything else happens we will, ok?"

"If anything else happens? He'll probably kill you next time! I mean look at you!"

Jane raised her hand to the cut on her forehead. She looked at the bruises on her arms and her legs. She traced the bruises on her face.

"I'll think about it. But… he's done something. I don't want to talk about it, but we can't tell anyone. It will get so

much worse if…" Jane couldn't bring herself to say it. She just wanted to cover up her newfound secret, which she would have to hide for who knew how long.

She would tell Poppy eventually, but she couldn't bring herself to do it now. "We need to act as if nothing has happened," she said firmly. "We don't want to start him off again."

Poppy swallowed, on the verge of tears herself. "Ok, fine! But I'm not letting you out of my sight, and that means Nico isn't letting either of us out of his sight, ok?"

"That's fine with me. Thanks for finding me." Jane nudged Poppy's side.

Poppy shook her head. "Yeah well, what can I say? You're pretty cool, and not to mention brave. Look at you, standing up to the bully of the school. Should do it more often, just need to have better timing," she said nudging Jane back.

Jane couldn't help but say ouch, which they both had a little laugh over. She looked at Jane back in the mirror before speaking again.

"Let's clean ourselves up, then. Can't let him win at everything, can we? Take your shirt off. We're swapping."

Jane looked down at her shirt. Fear gripped her again. She hadn't even noticed the stains of blood all over it. She imagined having been in the bed with Jack slinking his fingers under her top. She had to get it off NOW! Without having to be asked twice, she took it off, and Poppy handed over her shirt. It was a crop top, and Jane grimaced at the idea of her bare midriff. She wanted to cover herself up as much as she could.

Jane watched Poppy put on her top, unbuttoning a few buttons at the bottom and twisting it around, making a knot. It covered most of the stains. She helped Jane wash out her cut.

"If anyone asks, we'll tell people we were doing a workout together, and as I was doing high knees, you went down to pick up your water bottle, and I kneed you in the eye."

Jane stared at her, and Poppy shrugged. "That's the best I've got right now. We'll figure out the rest if people ask."

Poppy took Jane's hair down, arranging it so she could hide behind it. She grabbed Jane's hand and opened the bathroom door. They walked down the stairs to the party.

Poppy hooked her arm through Jane's. She grabbed a couple of red plastic cups and filled them with an unknown beverage. Jane planned to tip hers out into the nearest houseplant. Thankfully the bluey purple lights helped her camouflage her bruises, so she shouldn't get too many questions.

Jane saw Nico across the room in the corner, talking to someone on the phone. He looked worried, but Poppy dragged Jane away. They took a seat on the couch next to Julie and Brittany who had dolled up for this "special" occasion. Jane felt like she was in a den of snakes. Her throat tightened, and she felt strangled as her classmates partied around her, oblivious. The people she'd thought were her friends didn't seem like they were anymore.

Julie and Brittany gossiped about a fight that happened today after school. It seemed that no one knew what actually happened. Jane tipped some of her drink into a plant next to her and wrapped her arms around herself. Poppy noticed her discomfort and changed the subject.

Jane tried to join in, but she still felt so spaced out. She kept thinking back to what happened. Pellets of sweat dripped down her back, and she wasn't even hot. In fact, she felt the opposite. All the windows and doors were open letting a cold wind come in.

Nico came up from behind them, leaning over and giving Poppy a peck on the lips. He patted Jane on the shoulder, making her flinch. Nico didn't seem to notice as he leaned down and whispered in her ear. "He's ok."

She turned to him, surprised, but he shook his head no, as in "will tell you later". Was he hiding the same secret as her? Did Jack already send a picture his way...? He dragged a chair up.

More and more of the gang wandered over. Tommy took a seat on the armrest next to Julie. He avoided looking at Jane. An awkward air surrounded him, and Jane was relieved to see some guilt in his expression. Perhaps he wasn't a complete sociopath after all. Sam and a few others joined the group and started to dance in the little circle they created.

Someone passed Jane a camera. She stared at it blankly for a moment, the events of the evening making her thoughts slow. She half-heartedly stood up, raising the camera and took a few shots. She thought back to the beach all those months ago. She felt more out of place now than back then.

Someone tapped her on the shoulder and held out their hand to have the camera. Gratefully, Jane handed it over, then she realized who it was. She turned around, taking a step back and bumped into Nico. He looked down at her with concern, then back to the new cameraman, Jack.

Jack smirked and raised the camera to look through the viewfinder. He took a photo and then another one. Jane tried to avoid the lens, but he kept focusing it on her, practically shoving the camera in her face. Didn't he already have enough photos of her?

Jane gave in. She stared directly into the lens, probably looking the most real she had in a while. The flash went off. He lowered it and looked down at the picture he'd taken. His expression froze, and he looked up, meeting Jane's eyes briefly, before she pulled her gaze away.

He stepped towards her and put the camera strap around her neck gently. He grabbed her hand, pulling her into the dance circle. He tried to get her to dance but she felt so stiff, she just stood there. She didn't want to be anywhere near him. Poppy came to her rescue, slipping in between them and wrapping her arms around Jane. They moved like a wave to the music. Jack stepped away but never stopped looking over towards them.

"I think I'm going to throw up. I want to leave." Jane said into Poppy's ear.

"You're ok, you're ok. Leaving now will make people suspicious." Poppy whispered, fiercely. "Don't let him win. If you stand strong, you can win in a way he doesn't think you can."

"Poppy, I can't..."

"You can! He broke you down, but he doesn't expect you to get up so fast. You're ok, fake it."

"It's more than that..." Jane whispered.

Poppy kept repeating the words "you're ok" and Jane started to believe her lie. She ignored the fact that she was sore and in an environment that she would never be comfortable in anyway. She started to dance, to relax... to go numb.

The atmosphere felt wild. Drinks were passed around and everything started to blur. She downed every cup that was handed to her, instead of feeding it to the plants. She didn't care anymore. The music grew louder, and Jane felt herself being handed around, dancing with a new partner every few minutes. None of their hands felt like Jack's hands, which she suspected was down to Nico and Poppy. Jane felt so appreciative towards them and made her way over to them.

They held her up, sharing a worried look. Jane tried to reassure them that she was ok, but instead heard herself yell the words "I'm so numb".

They helped her outside. The cold seemed to bring some sense back to her. The two of them mumbled back and forth to each other, and then Jack came up behind them.

Jane saw all of their faces staring at her. She sat on the wet ground, letting her hand roll over the grass. They muttered about who was going to take her home or something like that, and Jane really couldn't care less. She stood and started walking herself down the road, disappearing into pitch black.

*

For what felt like hours, Jane walked. She didn't know the way home, but eventually found a street that looked familiar.

She guessed walking around endlessly, drunk in the cold, had at least sobered her up a little.

She'd turned down so many wrong roads that she couldn't even remember where she'd started.

She looked up at the streetlamps. Her breath misted under the light, making her feel a new level of cold. She could see her house down the road, her mom's car still not there. She was working another double.

Jane snorted out loud. She wasn't surprised. Her mom had said she would be there for her more, but it was almost Christmas and not much had changed. She wouldn't even know what had happened unless Jane told her.

Someone else's car was parked in the drive. Jane's leaden feet dragged up the few porch steps and the sudden movement caused the security light to flicker on. Looking up to Theo's room, she saw his curtains were still open. She should go see if he's ok, or at least home.

Before she turned around to make her way to his place she bumped into her front door, making the Christmas wreath jingle. Footsteps padded across the floor behind the door. Jane froze. No one should be in her house.

She stumbled back, as the door opened. Warm air from inside rushed towards her, knocking her off balance. Her arms circled instinctively, but the fall seemed to last forever. She never hit the ground. Instead, she was being carried inside. Strong arms put her down on a soft cloud. She felt, rather than saw them rush away.

Jane went to call out to her savior, but something stopped her. Her eyes shifted, taking in bags on the floor. New bags. One with a camo pattern on it.

A rush of footsteps came towards her and something cold and wet pressed against her head. Jane squirmed away, but the strong arms were back, holding her still.

She followed them up to their shoulders, then to their neck. Up, up, up, she found a stranger looking back at her, but his smell was familiar. He stroked her hair back, tears brimming in his eyes. He blinked rapidly, trying to make them go away, only resulting in making it worse.

Jane raised her hand and touched his cheek. Stubble brushed against her fingers. "Will?"

He nodded and held her closer. Jane had forgotten what his hugs felt like.

"I'm sorry," she said as she melted into his warmth. She heard him shush her. But Jane couldn't stop. She felt herself repeat her apology over and over, until she was too tired to move her mouth. With his warmth and the darkness, she couldn't fight it any longer. She let them both consume her.

20.

Theo

The photo burned into Theo's mind; he couldn't stop thinking about it. About her. Where was she? Nico said she was at the party, but surely she would have left? Unless Jack was already threatening her with the photo.

Theo had sent her message after message, but still nothing. He wondered whether she even had her phone anymore. Maybe she'd dropped it during the fight.

Theo sat on his bed, looking directly out of his window into hers, hoping she would appear at some point. Two hours of sitting there, and the only change was an anemone petal falling, landing on the windowsill.

Other than that, nothing. He fell back on his bed, giving in to sleep.

*

Light beamed into the bedroom, hitting the floor. Slowly it moved further and further up Theo's body, finally reaching his eyes. A few seconds of it shining in his face was all Theo needed to be woken up. Raising his hand to cover his eyes, he groaned with the sudden movement.

Had he broken something? Probably some ribs. He struggled to sit up. He got one arm underneath himself and pushed himself upright. Glancing around the room, he saw the chair shoved under the door handle, and memories of what had happened came back to him.

There was a note on the floor, slipped under the door. His mom must have tried to come in, but in the chair had kept her out. Shards of glass glistened on the carpet. Rainbow patterns stretched from them. His eyes followed one up the wall, reaching his windowsill.

Jane. He stared out towards her window. The only thing different was that it looked like she was on her bed, asleep.

141

He stood, picking his way around the glass, and squinted, trying to get a closer look. It must be her.

Jane's door opened and Will walked in. He sat down next to her, pushing her hair back a little, before getting up. He left the room, closing the door behind him.

After a few minutes, he came out the front door with a bunch of reusable bags and hopped into his car. Theo watched as he reversed out of their driveway and drove away. Will must've been going to the grocery store.

Theo ran his hands down his face. Jane was alone, her mother's car was missing from the driveway, she was probably doing another double shift at the hospital.

Jane shouldn't be alone right now.

He turned and carefully picked his way to his door. Moving the chair, he grabbed the note, pausing to read it. It was just another one of his mother's emotional quotes. She sometimes slid them under his door when she thought he felt frustrated. It made him smile a little. They didn't work, but she kept putting in the effort. He placed it on his bedside table and turned to make his way out.

An ear-splitting shriek rang out behind him. He spun around. Jane picked something up and threw it across her room. She disappeared from his view as she bent to pick up something else. Theo stumbled out of his room, downstairs, out to his backyard and to their connecting gate, swinging it open and almost breaking it off its hinges. Reaching her back door, he swung it open and stepped inside. He didn't stop to look around as he took the stairs two at a time. Another noise came from a closed door – Jane's door.

"Jane?" He cracked the door open, an inch at first, making sure she knew someone was coming in. Once he was sure she wasn't going to throw something at him, he pushed it open, revealing her.

He almost cried at the sight of her. Bruises traced all over her arms, her neck, and one across her cheek. A Band-Aid was pressed over her forehead, covering what he assumed was a gash from Jack knocking her unconscious. Her eye was

swollen. Her hair stuck to her face, tears streaking her cheeks. She stood staunch, unsure of her own movements, as her hand gripped the candle – the next victim that was about to be thrown before Theo had appeared.

She was wearing a crop top and jeans – the top was different from the one she'd had on yesterday, but otherwise she hadn't bothered changing. She reeked of alcohol.

They stared at each other for a moment before Jane dropped the candle on the bed and dashed towards him. She hugged him as tightly as she could. He hugged her just as tight in return.

He stepped into her room still enclosed in her arms. He found the door handle behind him and closed it. Hearing her sniffle, he squeezed her tighter. His eyes darted around the room, noticing broken glass on her floor too. He stepped back, moving them away from it.

Suddenly, Jane let go, pushing herself away from him. Confused, he reached out to her again, but stopped just short of touching her. Fear seemed to capture both of them and she took another step back.

"Jane?"

"I can't do this." She looked down at her feet, crossing her arms over her chest.

Theo shook his head. "Do what?"

"You know… this." She gestured to the space in between them. She was hiding something.

"What do you mean?" Theo took a step back in surprise.

"I… we can't risk it anymore. Jack will notice. And he… he…" She looked up at him, her eyes filling. "I thought you were dead, Theo," she whispered. "I can't lose you."

"You'll lose me by pushing me away."

Jane swallowed. "I can't do this right now."

Theo swallowed. "I know what he has over you."

Jane looked away, unable to meet his eye. Theo hated seeing that look. She had nothing to be ashamed of, it was all on Jack.

"I wish I'd come to the party and taken you home, but Nico told me not to…" Theo took a hesitant step towards her. "I can't lose you, Jane."

"You know what he did?"

"Nico told me what he did, what he… took. He must've told Nico, knowing that he would message me, so I wouldn't do anything."

Jane stepped back speechless until she backed onto a piece of glass. She cried out reaching forward to Theo. Theo caught her, bundling her into his arms. He sat them down on the edge of the bed. He raised her foot, inspecting it. A small shard of glass stuck out from her skin.

Before he had time to ask whether he could pull it out, Jane shook her head, violently. "He'll ruin me. He'll show everyone the photos."

Theo froze. Photos? Plural? He took more than one?

"That asshole."

"There's nothing we can do." She looked at Theo, now leaning on her arms, bracing herself. She nodded her head as he returned his attention to the piece of glass. He gripped it and quickly pulled it out. Jane cried out, instinctively flinching away from him. Theo saw an old shirt on the ground and wrapped it around her foot. He wanted to bandage it properly, but he couldn't leave her. She moved back to him, sitting beside him on the edge of the bed.

There was a little space between them. His hand was no longer on her foot but resting next to her, there for her if she wanted it, but he didn't want to force anything on her.

Silence surrounded them for a moment. Theo listened to her shaky breaths. After a moment, she took his hand and squeezed it, but her breathing changed, becoming short, quickened gasps.

Theo turned to her, and she looked at him with pure panic in her eyes. Tears streamed downed her cheeks, and she seemed to struggle to get another breath in. He moved off the bed, crouching in front of her, still gripping her hand. Her other hand grabbed at her throat.

"Are you choking?" Theo practically yelled the words. She shook her head, opening her mouth to speak. No words came out, and she pulled her hand away from him. Shit, she was having a panic attack. Her whole body trembled.

Theo's hands reached up to cup her face, making her focus completely on him. "Jane, you're having a panic attack. I've had many, ok? Just breathe, just breathe, please! Jane!"

She slithered down off the bed into his arms. Her skin burned hot against his. Tears edged at Theo's eyes. He didn't know what else to do. He leaned down, planting his lips on hers. Her eyes widened with surprise, then closed and she kissed him back.

Milliseconds passed and they broke apart. She finally breathed out and in rapidly, but in a calmer manner.

"I don't want to be his," she said, tears freely streaming. "I want to be yours."

The words almost broke Theo. "You shouldn't have to be anyone's," he said.

He moved her into a more comfortable position, his arms wrapped tighter around her. He listened to her sobs. That's all he could do; that's all he should do. So, as she sobbed, Theo rocked both of them together.

21.

Jane

Theo held Jane for hours, never complaining about his tear-soaked shirt or legs cramping where she leaned on them. Even when she tried to stop crying, new waves of tears would break inside her, and she'd cuddle into Theo again.

He didn't say anything, and she was glad of that. She just wanted to be held, and that's all he did. The panic attack had made her feel like her throat was closing up, like she had forgotten how to breathe. When he kissed her, she felt like her heart had been restarted. She had never felt so much urgency and passion in a kiss before, and she craved more of it.

A few hours later, they heard someone come in the front door. Jane and Theo looked at each other. She felt herself start to panic, as flashbacks of the night before overwhelmed her.

"Jane? Are you up? I bought you some snacks."

They both relaxed at the sound of Will's voice. Theo let out a sigh of relief. She looked at him, confused. He didn't know who it was, did he? As if he could read her mind, he answered her puzzled expression.

"We met last night," he said sheepishly. "I came over, looking for you."

Jane swallowed. Theo really cared about her. If she let him go, she would be an idiot.

"Should we go downstairs?" he asked.

Jane nodded. He grabbed her hand and stood up, helping her in the process. Her foot hurt to walk on, but it was just a little cut. Theo winced as she leaned on him, and she wondered if he was hurting even more than she was.

Even so, walking downstairs felt like a mammoth task. She found herself leaning on him, and he supported her weight despite the pain it must have been causing him.

146

They sat down on the breakfast bar stools. Will had his back to them and was busy unpacking the endless groceries he'd brought. Jane couldn't remember the last time they had this much food in the house. He muttered under his breath about how they survived like this. "We did have food," she said. "The essentials."

This got a laugh out of him and a smile from Theo. Her mom hadn't done a proper shop for a few weeks, and Jane had to admit, she'd had to make do with some strange meals recently.

Will turned around to face her, his face darkening as he took in Theo. "Who's this?" Will didn't bother with pleasantries or trying to sound polite. He looked Theo up and down, his posture hardening.

"This is Theo. He lives next door. You met him last night, remember? He came over asking for me."

"I remember. Jane was at some party, huh?" Will moved closer to Theo, his eyes blazing.

Theo went to stand, but Will moved in the way. Theo sat back, pressing himself into the benchtop behind him. Jane noticed he was trying to get as far away from Will as he could. Sweat had formed on his forehead and his eyes started to dart around in a panic.

Jane grabbed Will's shoulder. "Will, stop. He helped me."

"Is that why he has matching bruises?" Will's eyes didn't move from Theo. "Did you do this? You think it's ok to hit girls? To hit my sister?"

Theo's breath caught as if he was about to have a panic attack. This sudden confrontation and being in a new environment was proving too much for him. Tears welled up in his eyes as his expression turned into a puppy dog's one.

Jane stood, getting in between them. "Will, stop, that's not what happened." Jane turned around to Theo. "It's ok, he's just being protective, just breathe. Do you need to go outside?" Theo swallowed down his apparent fear and wiped at his eyes.

"No, no it's ok. I'm just overwhelmed. I think I'll be fine."

"Oh yeah?" Will looked between them, his gaze hardening every time it landed on Theo.

"Back off, Will."

"I will, once you start telling me what happened."

Jane swallowed. "Ok, ok, I'll tell you the truth. But you can't tell anyone, Will. I don't want people to know what happened."

Will frowned. He took a step away, backing off from Theo. He folded his arms, his posture relaxing slightly. Jane took a breath and looked to Theo, who gave her a little nod of encouragement. She noticed him drawing in breath after breath, silently holding each one as if he was doing a breathing exercise.

"I did go to a party… but I was forced to."

Will's frown deepened. "Forced to… What do you mean? By who? Him?"

"No, I would never!" Theo looked genuinely horrified at the idea. He was so different to Jack.

"No, not Theo. There's this guy at school…" Jane paused, wondering how she could possibly explain everything that had happened. "He has to have everything his way, and he's been kind of intense with me."

"He's a possessive maniac," Theo cut in. "I was trying to help her."

"Well, it doesn't seem like you did a very good job." Will's eyes were still hard, but he was no longer in Theo's personal space.

"Just shush and let me explain." Jane's patience was wearing thin. "It all started after our English practice test. I was walking with Theo to his art class when Tommy grabbed me from behind and pushed me around the corner, handing me off to Jack, who basically dragged me around the back of the gym. He must've planned it or something since it was a spot no one would come across." Jane took a breather, the events starting to overwhelm her again. "And then he pushed me back into the wall and started to argue with me about how I hadn't been very present lately. I could see him getting

angrier, so I tried to get out of there when I heard Theo coming. I didn't make it very far and we both fell over. He wouldn't get off and that's when Theo appeared. Theo got a few good punches in, but it didn't last long. He knocked Theo nearly unconscious when I stepped in. I didn't want Theo to get hurt anymore so I let go of him." She turned her head to Theo who was watching her. She felt ashamed about letting go, but he took her hand and gave it a gentle squeeze. "Then Jack hauled me away and knocked me out since I wasn't cooperating, obviously," she touched the bandage on her forehead.

"Then I woke up at the party. I got drunk and walked home." She abruptly ended her story, not wanting tell Will about the pictures unless she had to.

Will's grip had tightened around his folded arms the more Jane explained. His hand slid down to his pocket once she had finished. He pulled out his phone.

"What are you doing?" Jane asked.

"Calling the cops."

Jane reached out to grab the phone, but Will held his arm in the air, keeping the phone out of her reach. To Jane's surprise, Theo jumped up, grabbed the phone, and ran off with it. He swore, as Will chased after him.

Jane tried to follow, but a sudden weakness overran her, and she fell to the ground.

"Will! Help!"

Will came back, quickly kneeling beside Jane, helping her up.

"Your pussy boyfriend locked himself in the guest bathroom."

Jane almost laughed out loud. Will helped Jane over to the bathroom door. He slammed his fists against it. "Get out here, Theo!"

Jane put her ear to the door.

"Sorry, that was my little sister. She didn't mean to call emergency services."

This time Jane did laugh, considering he didn't even have a little sister. She slid down to the ground, sitting by the door. Theo unlocked and opened it. He raised his hands, clearly scared Will might hit him. Will grabbed his arm, swinging him out of the bathroom.

"Give me my phone."

Theo just shrugged, raising his empty hands again. Will shook his head, shoving Theo aside. He ripped through the bathroom, looking for the phone.

Theo sat down beside Jane, gently placing the phone in her lap.

"Thank you," Jane mouthed to him.

Will gave a frustrated groan and came out of the bathroom. He closed the door, then slid down it and joined them on the ground. He leaned back, hitting the door behind him.

"But why? You need to talk to the police. This dude is dangerous. He almost killed both of you from the sounds of it."

Snippets of the night came back to Jane and she reached out, squeezing Theo's hand. He squeezed back.

"I just don't want the police involved, ok?" Jane knew it wasn't a good answer.

"What about you? What do you think?" Will looked to Theo.

Theo didn't look up. "It's her choice. And whatever she decides, I have to be fine with, even if I don't agree. It happened to her. Not me."

Will shook his head. "But you got hurt too."

Theo shrugged. "Because I was trying to help her. What did I expect? That I would beat Jack?"

"Jack?" Will raised his eyebrows. "So that's his name?"

"Theo!"

"Sorry, I didn't mean to." Theo lowered his gaze again.

Jane sighed. "Look, I don't want this blown up more than it has. I don't want Jack to leak the…" Jane cut herself off, shame filling her.

"Leak what? What aren't you telling me?" Will's temper rose again.

Jane swallowed, nausea filling her stomach. "At the party, when I was still unconscious, he took some... revealing photos of me. He said he'll send them out to everyone if I say anything. He'll tell everyone I wanted him so bad that I sent him photos." Jane's hands shook. She couldn't believe she'd just told Will that. It was bad enough the photos existed, let alone her brother knowing about them.

"We are definitely calling the police now!"

"He said that to you?" Theo added in.

"Will, you can't! Look, there's only a few more months left until our last year at school ends, so I'm just going to stick it out. If I just keep quiet, nothing will happen." Jane didn't quite believe what she was saying.

"So you're just going to pretend nothing happened? Go back to how it was before? How?" Theo was shaking, all of it catching up to him.

Jane's heart hurt for him when she heard his voice break in disbelief. "It's the only thing I can do. If I don't... I guess that's my chances gone for getting into a good college and finding a job. I'll be known as another girl who sends nudes, even if it isn't true," she said quietly.

"I need to think about this." Will rubbed his mouth, his anger barely contained behind it. "But I swear Jane, if you turn up like you did this morning again, I will find Jack and kill him myself, got it?"

Jane nodded, not doubting his words.

"And I'm not making any promises. I still might call the cops myself." Will got up, walking back into the kitchen. A second later, Jane heard him unpacking the groceries again, or at least slamming the cupboards. It would be a miracle if the food made it into the pantry unscathed.

Theo made a move to stand too. He held out his hand to help Jane get up but never looked directly at her.

"Do you want to come out and get some fresh air with me?" Theo asked, Jane nodded.

They walked outside together. Theo helped Jane sit down on the top step, but when he sat, he left a gap in between them, a noticeable space. Jane shivered, forgetting how cold it was. Theo glanced at her and took off his sweater, handing it over. Jane slipped it on, smelling his scent in it. She went to put her hand on his shoulder, but he flinched away.

"Don't, Jane," he mumbled.

"Don't what?"

He stood and walked down the few steps. He raised his hands, letting them rest on his head. His shirt lifted, revealing a peek of his toned abdomen, and a yellow, greenish bruise appearing under his shirt. He let out a sharp breath before taking another shaky one in.

"Are you ok?"

"No!" Theo let his hands drop to his sides. "I'm not alright. I worried about you the whole night. When I came over to you, you were in tears. You looked afraid of me. I would never hurt you. Never. And… and… I just can't get my head around you wanting to go back to hanging out with him. Do I even matter to you?" He took another shaky breath. "I just don't get it. How could you? I don't understand. What are we? What is this?" He looked at Jane, his eyes pleading.

"Theo, I'm so sorry. I didn't mean to drag you into all this. Believe me, I don't ever want to be near him again. But I feel like if I don't, then he'll start sending those pictures to everyone. If I can just hold on until summer, he won't be able to threaten me anymore. We will all be going our separate ways." Jane looked at Theo. He looked like he was on the edge of a breakdown. "And yes, of course you matter. I really like you. You don't know how thankful I am for you."

"But why do you have to go back to him?"

Jane wrung her hands together, twisting her fingers, before looking up at Theo. His face had changed, concern filling it. He sat back down next to her.

"I just told you why, but last night…" Jane's voice cracked just thinking about it. She took a breath, steeling herself. "When I woke up, I was in a bed with Jack. And he threatened

to do worse if I acted out again. He told me I was his, and only his… I'm scared Theo."

Swearing under his breath, Theo put an arm around Jane's shoulders. She rested her head on his shoulder. "This isn't right. You know that though, don't you?"

"I know and I'm sorry. I don't feel like I have any other choice."

"Well, if that's how you feel… ok then. But I'm not going to let you out of my sight. Well, I'll try not to… and Nico and Poppy will help with that, I'm sure."

Jane looked up at him, and he looked down, their eyes locking. He leaned down and kissed Jane softly, tenderly. They broke apart and he stood again. Jane didn't want him to leave.

"I'll be back for my sweater." Winking, he backed away and walked back through the open gate, not bothering to close it. Jane wrapped her arms around herself, feeling his presence through his sweater.

A car door slammed, making Jane jump. Her mom must be home, finally. What kind of story was Jane going to have to sell once her mom saw her?

22.

Theo

They hung out most of the Christmas break. Theo was even invited around for Jane's family's Christmas Eve meal. Jane's mother and brother acted warmly towards him, which he was thankful for. Will seemed to have kept his promise not to tell anyone.

Thankfully, both of their bruises had faded by the time Christmas came around. Theo still groaned quietly to himself and had to excuse himself whenever his ribs were playing up. He'd go to the bathroom and basically teach himself how to breathe again. Once when Jane came over, looking for him, she found him in agony on the bathroom floor. He watched her face and almost thought she was going to run the other way, but she kneeled gently next to him and sat quietly while he tried to breathe.

When Christmas actually hit, he felt panicked. He hadn't thought to get her anything, completely forgetting about it. So the night of their dinner, he went home and drew her some purple anemones. He added a couple of butterflies, monarchs. He felt like it was appropriate, since it was what started everything off. He found an old frame to put it in and messaged her to meet him outside. He got a reply in seconds.

WHAT DO YOU MEAN, "MEET ME OUTSIDE"?

Theo chuckled at the reply, but he was already outside. He walked towards her gate, leaving her on read. He thought about replying but that might have ruined his chances of her coming outside in the icy temperature.

He sidestepped around a patch of ice and waited down by her back steps. He hadn't really thought this through, but he couldn't back out now. He heard someone unlock the back door. She stepped out, causing the sensor light to turn on. She walked down the steps, looking sleepily frustrated.

"Theo, it's 3 a.m.," she said groggily, making him smile.

"Merry Christmas!" he replied, enthusiastically.

"I've never been up this early for Christmas. Ever."

"I know! Same! Isn't it great?"

"Theodore…"

"Janieee…"

"What do you have there?" Smiling at him, she gave him a friendly bump.

"Merry Christmas, Jane," he said once again, handing over his present. He didn't even think to wrap it. He awkwardly looked down now, feeling embarrassed. He scratched his head. He instinctively wanted to rock, but the thought passed as he witnessed Jane's reaction.

She surprised him by reaching out and hugging him. He wrapped his arms around her. He felt her head tuck into the crook of his neck.

"I love it," she stood on her tippy toes whispering into his ear. Theo had to catch his tongue, almost confessing his love for her right then and there.

He let go of her. "I have another present for you."

"Oh yeah? What is it?" she said, mischievously looking up at him and closing the space in-between them. He gently took her face in his hands and kissed her. They broke apart, resting their foreheads against each other, breathing the same air.

"Can I be your girlfriend?" whispered Jane.

He looked down at her in complete awe. "One hundred percent yes! Of course… but what about school?"

She shrugged. "We'll work it out."

For today at least, they could live in the moment. Neither of them said anything.

He leaned down and kissed her again. "Goodnight, Jane." He let go of her and made his way towards their gate. Before crossing into his backyard, he stopped and looked back at the girl that changed his life.

"That was the best gift I've ever been given."

*

Jane

Jane replayed the moment they had shared early Christmas morning, hundreds of times. It made her feel safe and loved whenever she thought about it. His words felt like words from an angel, and they gave her so much warmth. It radiated out of her in her everyday tasks.

Over the rest of their Christmas break, they had come up with a plan for their last semester at school. Theo seemed annoyed that she had to hang out with her group, but neither of them could figure out a way to avoid it that didn't result in Jack leaking the pictures.

For the whole of January their plan worked perfectly. Once school had finished and they were both at home, they were inseparable. They either hung out in her living room, in his backyard, or sometimes at his house.

Jane had gone to a few dinners at his place and noticed his dad was looking better. Will was deployed again shortly after Christmas break was over, but he promised to stay in touch this time. He made it very clear that he expected regular updates. He'd even warmed up to Theo a bit, which she was grateful for.

Her mom couldn't be more delighted to hear about them being together. She still took double shifts though and continued with her therapy, so perhaps she was just happy that someone else was keeping Jane company.

Theo kept his word – Jane was never alone at school. Either Poppy or Nico were always next to her when they were in a group setting, and Jane could almost always sense Theo close by.

Not much changed other than that really. Jack was his usual arrogant self, except she could tell he was aware of her distancing. Jane could see his brain ticking over, trying to figure out a way to talk to her or even get near her. She tried to act as normal as she could, but he made her uneasy and she thought some of the others in the group had noticed that too. She didn't want to do anything wrong, but she couldn't help becoming a nervous wreck when he appeared.

Jane couldn't believe her last year at high school was finishing so soon. Her last four months were going to be filled with assignments and tests until summer started. Then she was free, until she went to college… if she got in that was.

One assignment she was particularly looking forward to was in the last month of school. It was the geography overnight field trip. They'd been building to it all year, and her teacher had given them all the paperwork and permission slips that morning.

It was going to be in their local woods. They would have to do a field work report about the environment out there. They also had to include a little bit of astronomy into their report. The weather forecast was supposed to be clear all day and night, so Jane was mostly looking forward to testing out her photography skills, taking photos of the sky. Another cool thing about it was that since they were in their last year they were given more 'space', meaning their teacher didn't have to be present the whole time. But she would do a few check-ups on them throughout the night.

Sadly, Theo didn't take geography so he couldn't come with her. He would have loved every bit about the trip, but instead, Nico would sleep in his tent alone and Poppy would be her tent buddy.

During lunch, word had spread about the field trip. It was a problem. Usually her group would go for their annual camping trip on the same weekend. This meant there wouldn't be a camping trip this year. Not everyone was upset, and Jane especially had been dreading the thought of having to go camping with Jack.

"Who doesn't take geography, raise your hand." Brittany said, her hand raised first. Then Sarah, Julie, Lucas, and Duke's hands followed. That left Sam, Tommy, Nico, Poppy, Jane, and Jack. Jack? When did Jack start taking geography? Her heart dropped. He must be in the other class.

"Ok, well you guys enjoy your lame school trip and we'll organize our own camping trip." Brittany said.

"Sure, yeah, whatever." Sam said. Jane felt the group split into two as everyone started talking about carpools and tent buddies.

Since Jane and Poppy were the only girls in their group, they had already made it clear that they would be tenting together. And that Poppy, Nico, and Jane would be going in the same car since they were all in the same class. Jack had tried to squeeze his way in, which made Jane anxious, but Poppy wasn't having a bar of that. She told him they couldn't fit another person in with all the gear.

Even so, Jane's stomach churned, knowing they would still have to go camping with him. But that was in three months' time. There was no point in overthinking it yet anyway.

The lunch bell rang and they all broke up to go to their different classes. Jane got stuck thinking about the field trip again, sighing out loud. She felt defeated.

*

"Ms Davidson, something the matter?"

Jane's thoughts got sliced in half in a blink of an eye. Her eyes widened, and she looked around at her classmates. Her mind had been completely on the trip again, despite the fact that she was in the middle of a lesson.

"Ms Davidson?"

The teacher asked again.

"Sorry Miss, I blanked out for a second. A lot on my mind. Sorry, I'll concentrate now."

The teacher looked at Jane, disappointed, but continued her lesson. Jane put her head down and noticed how many doodles she had done on her page while she was thinking. She ripped the page off and started again.

She copied the notes from the board as fast as she could before they got rubbed off. Jane felt a tap on her shoulder and turned around to Jack mouthing, "Daydreamer Jane". She turned back without giving him anything in return.

This was the only class she had where she was alone with Jack. It put her on edge which was probably what was making her overthink. It was also probably why she was doing badly in this class. She could never think clearly with him around.

The spot where he'd tapped her on the shoulder burned. She gave it a rub to try and get rid of his touch. She was completely vulnerable.

The class thankfully continued with no other dramas – no other interruptions from Jack – and in half an hour the bell rang. Jane packed her stuff away and headed out of the room.

She'd spoke too soon. A familiar burning feeling wrapped around her shoulders. She shoved Jack off, but he came right back.

"Whoa, whoa, whoa, dreamer. Where are you off to so fast?" Jack said coolly.

She looked around the hall, seeing no one familiar. She knew Jack would find the perfect time to strike. She was all alone.

"What do you want, Jack?" she said, snapping back.

He chuckled, following her to her next class. "Someone didn't feed the pussy cat today?"

Jane sped up. Walking faster was the only thing she could do. Jack ran ahead and sidestepped, stopping her in her tracks.

"What are you so worried about? I ain't going to do anything…" he turned his voice to a whisper and leaned in and continued "Not here anyway. I know what you and your little gang are doing. Remember what I have."

Jane's breath caught in her throat. She looked straight ahead and saw the door to her next class open and close as students went in and out. So close, but yet, so far.

"You coming?" he said casually.

Jane stared at him, confused. "Coming where?"

"Camping. Where else, dreamer?" Winking at her, he smirked.

"If you weren't listening at lunchtime, yes, I am. It's a school assignment!" Jane said lifting her arms in the air in a gesture of frustration and storming past him. Pushing on the door of her next class, she looked back to him standing in the middle of the hall. Students swirled around him, and he looked absolutely gobsmacked. He wanted a challenge, but she had made it easy for him.

*

After school, Jane helped Theo out in his garden. They had made a lot of progress and some of the flowers they had planted were starting to bloom. To Theo's excitement, they had also sighted a few butterflies and bees.

"Do the butterflies in your stomach have a name?" she joked. She paused, waiting for Theo's reply, but he hadn't been very talkative the whole evening.

"Belly-flies, butter-stomach… crippling nerves. That's a good name, isn't it? Theo?"

Jane turned around, waiting for him to joke with her, but he looked directly at her.

"How can you go?"

"Go where?"

"Camping."

Jane's heart dropped. How'd he find out? Jane had planned on telling him closer to the time.

"Nico told me," he added, as if she'd spoken the thought aloud.

That made sense. They were pretty good buds now, always running and hanging out, which Jane was thankful for. It was nice for him to have another friend.

She sighed. "I was going to tell you."

"When?" he shot back.

"Closer to the time. It's ok, calm down."

"I am calm."

"That's what hysterical people say," Jane said, teasing to try and make it less of a situation.

Theo couldn't help but grin. He made his way over to Jane and wrapped his arms around her. "I can't keep you safe if you go."

"You're not always going to be able to keep me safe, and anyway it's a field trip. There will be teachers around."

"I would like to come though. The teachers won't be around all the time." Theo gently tucked his head into the crook of Jane's neck like a lost puppy. "I want to keep you safe, I mean."

"It'll be ok." Jane didn't want to argue anymore. She felt Theo nod against her, but he held her tighter. "It'll be ok," she whispered this time more to convince herself than anyone else.

## 23

## Theo

A few weeks had passed since they had talked about Jane's field trip and spring had arrived. Nothing much had changed. They still hung out every evening after school. School was busy, getting them ready for their tests. Theo still didn't feel certain about Jane going on the trip, but he couldn't stop her. He couldn't do anything actually. It was for a school assignment and she couldn't not go. It was too late for him to join the class – not that he wanted to study geography anyway. He just had to accept the fact she was going camping, and Jack was going to be there too.

Late one Saturday afternoon, he hadn't seen Jane all day. They had messaged back and forth a few times but otherwise, nothing. He was itching to go and see her, but he didn't want to appear too needy. She had mentioned that she was studying for the tests coming up, but Theo thought she studied too much. Maybe he should go over there and just see her? The thought made him nervous, just barging in like that, but he missed her. He'd only barged in once before, but he'd had a good enough reason for that.

He sent a quick message.

I'M COMING OVER, I MISS YOU.

Which he hoped she would see before he arrived. This was to help settle his own thoughts, so he wasn't being completely rude. Without getting caught up in his overthinking spiral, he grabbed a sweater and jogged down the stairs. His mom was sitting on the couch watching Holiday Home. His dad was asleep next to her. He looked more exhausted than ever.

Dad still had cancer but apparently the chemo was working and they were close to getting rid of it, which was really good news.

"Mom," Theo whispered.

Her hand reached down to pause the TV. "Yes?" she whispered back.

"Can I borrow the car keys?"

Her eyebrows knitted together. "Why?"

"I want to take Jane out for a date." Her face lit up with surprise. It was probably the first time he had said that out loud. But then again, they hadn't been on a proper date ever, because of Jack's threat.

"Sure honey, but be back by ten."

That was fine with Theo since it was only 5 p.m. "Thanks, see you later."

"Love you."

"Love you too." He twisted around, grabbed the keys off the hook and quietly made his way out the back door. He trotted through the connecting gate and made his way up to Jane's deck. He took out his phone to see if she had replied, but she hadn't. Opening the door, he stepped inside. He inhaled heavily through his nose; the house always smelt like vanilla. It calmed his nerves.

Jane wasn't downstairs, so he took the stairs two at a time, then got to her door. There she was. Her head was stuck in a Geography book, her hair up in a messy bun, papers scattered all around her. She got more beautiful every time he saw her. He knocked quietly on the door frame. Her head shot up, her eyes filling with surprise.

"Theo? What are you doing here?" Her smile made the question sound less harsh.

"I thought we could go out…" he said hesitantly.

"Go out?"

"Yeah… go out?"

"Like 'go out' out?"

"Yes. Go out out."

"Ohh… go out out." Jane shot a mischievous grin in Theo's direction.

"So… you wanna come?"

"What about Jack? What if someone sees us?"

Theo thought this would come up, and he'd really had enough of Jack's threat. He wished he could steal Jack's phone and smash it to bits.

"He won't. We won't go anywhere too public. Anyway, doesn't he play football on Saturdays?"

"I think the season finished… but I could be wrong."

"Could have…" Theo shrugged.

"Oh what the hell! Let's do it. I think I deserve a break," Jane said, tossing her Geography book to the side and getting up out of her sea of papers.

"I think you do too." Theo said. He walked to Jane, bringing her in close.

"Oh, do you now?" Jane looked up at him. Theo closed the space in between them, the sweetness of her soft lips meeting his. Her lips were softer than anything Theo knew, like biting into cotton candy, or soft like a paint brush. His lips were her canvas. They were so sweet, so effortlessly sweet. The kiss lasted longer than he intended it to, but he wasn't complaining. He kissed down her neck, and little giggles escaped Jane before he broke away.

"I suppose I should get ready then," Jane said cheerfully.

"I suppose you should."

"I'll be five minutes, wait downstairs for me?"

"Sure." He gave her another peck on the lips before walking down to wait.

*

He didn't know how she could look any more beautiful. She wore a denim skirt and a stripy V-neck blouse that she had tucked in. The blouse had long sleeves and gave off a little bit of a bohemian vibe. Her hair was still up in a messy bun, but it suited the outfit. She also wore the white Doc Martens her mom had got her for Christmas. Clutched in her hands was a knitted cardigan and her phone.

"Cheese!" her phone was now aimed at Theo, the flash going off bringing him out of his daze. He instinctively covered his eyes with his arm.

"You're supposed to smile, silly." She raised her phone again. This time Theo was ready. He gave her a big smile. He couldn't help it, he had the most gorgeous photographer.

"Your turn!" he held out his hand. Jane placed her phone in his palm. He started taking photos of her as she gave him a shy smile. He turned the phone onto selfie mode, put his arm around her middle and brought her in close. She giggled, and they both looked at the camera and took a few more.

"You ready?" he said, handing her phone back just as a message from Jack came through on their group chat. The urge to rock tugged at him, but he resisted. It was just something about the fact that Jack was messaging Jane when they were together. Of course, Jack didn't know… or did he? Guilt crept over Theo at putting Jane in danger. She didn't seem to notice or feel similar.

"Yep!"

"Let's go then!" He shook off the feeling. Jack couldn't know. It took everything in his power to take Jane's hand, give her a warm smile, and go out the front door and just forget about it.

On their way they listened to everything from Taylor Swift to Eminem as Jane surfed through her playlist. She danced in the passenger seat while Theo kept his focus on the road. He didn't want to tell her that the music, the road noise, her singing, other cars all around them, and her dancing was a lot for him to be taking in all at once. Theo thought he could handle it all at the moment, and he didn't want her to stop dancing. Anyway, they were almost at their destination.

He pulled into the local diner's parking lot, and put the car in neutral, switching off the engine.

Jane looked around. "I thought you said not a public place."

"It isn't, well… it's not very busy. And where else are we gonna go?"

"Hmmm, I don't know…"

He could see Jane's nerves rising. "How about we can just get the meal as takeout and go eat it at the local lookout?" he suggested. Jane's nerves were making his return.

"Ok… ok, I'm good with that."

He squeezed her hand and they hopped out of the car. He waited for her to come around to his side of the car and he went to grab her hand, but she folded her arms. Annoyance struck him. Not towards her – towards Jack. Why did he have to be such a dick?

They walked inside. A few locals were around, but none of them did a double take. Theo and Jane walked up to the counter and waited until the waitress came up.

"Hiya honeys, how can I help you?"

"Is it ok if we get our order to go?" Jane spoke for the both of them.

"Sure, what would'cha like?"

"I'll have a hamburger, fries, and a chocolate shake…" Jane looked at Theo, he hesitated, panicking all of a sudden.

"I'll have the same," he blurted out, not bothering to read the menu board.

Jane leaned over and whispered in his ear. "You don't like pickles in your burger though…"

"With no pickles please," he added.

"Sure, coming right up! Are we splitting the check or…?"

"No, no, I'm paying," Theo said, he stepped around Jane who already had her card out. He quickly tapped his before she could.

"Right, thanks, sweethearts. Just take a seat in a booth; it'll be done in about ten minutes."

They both said thanks and took a seat. Jane sat next to the window and Theo slid into the seat next to her. He placed his hand in hers under the table. They people-watched for a few minutes.

Then Theo saw Jack. He ripped his hand out of Jane's grasp and stood up. Shit. Was it really Jack or did he just think he'd seen him? Was he just imagining things?

"What is it?" Jane hissed at him, her eyes looking around wildly. "Theo?"

"… A bee, sorry." He didn't want to spook her. He sat back down next to her.

"Are you serious? You're surrounded by bees daily. In your garden."

"This one was a big bee."

"Oh… whatever." She rolled her eyes in his direction seeing right through the lie. Theo had just started to relax when he thought he saw Jack again. Instead of hopping up, he gripped the seat beneath him. He swung his legs instead of rocking his whole body.

"Ouch!" Jane yelped. Theo had kicked her.

"Shit! I'm sorry!"

"What is up with you?"

He opened his mouth to answer, but the waitress called out, cutting him off.

"Two hamburgers, one no pickle, fries and chocolate shakes!"

Jane moved out of the booth and walked up to the counter. Theo walked slowly behind her. He looked out the window, and there was Jack again! A coldness wrapped around him, overtaking him. His hands started to shake and sweat trickled down his back. Jane passed him the food. She stared at him, her concern growing as she absorbed his appearance and without saying anything, she placed a hand on his back and guided him outside. They reached the car slowly. Theo unlocked it and they hopped in.

Shit. Jack definitely would have seen them now. What would he do? It was all Theo's fault too. He couldn't stop himself from rocking slightly back and forth.

Jane took the food from him. "Theo, what's wrong?"

"We are done for Jane," he mumbled.

"What do you mean?"

"Jack. He's here." Theo watched as Jane whipped her head around, looking everywhere.

"Where? Where did you see him?" Panic coursed through her voice.

"Outside, near the dumpsters. Shit. I am so sorry, Jane. What is he going to do? I can't let him do anything to you. I won't. Shhhiii…"

Jane stared towards the dumpsters. Her eyebrows slowly crept down into a frown. "Where?" she asked again.

Theo couldn't look; he just pointed.

Jane went quiet. "Isn't that just the kitchen hand?" she asked finally.

Theo's rocking stalled. He took his head out of his hands. "What?"

"Over there? Was that who you saw? It's not Jack."

Theo followed Jane's pointed finger. She was right, it wasn't Jack. "Oh."

"You're seeing things."

"Mmm." Theo looked down, suddenly feeling ashamed. It should have been Jane freaking out, but he had done that for her.

"It's ok, Theo. He's not going to do anything to me. I'm right here."

"I'm so sorry."

"No! No, don't be. We both know what he has against me, so I think we are both a little on edge, that's all."

"Yeah, yeah, you're right. I've… I've just ruined our evening though." Guilt battled with the shame inside Theo.

"You're just looking out for me. It's ok… How about we go back to mine and just chill out there. We don't need to go anywhere else."

"You're right. Yeah, sure." Theo felt himself calming down.

"Are you sure you're ok to drive?"

"What? Are you offering to drive?" Theo chuckled. "You don't even know how."

"True, but I'm just asking."

"I'll be fine." Theo took a breath. He hadn't wanted to say anything before, but now he really needed to be able to focus. "But can we keep the music low this time, if that's ok?"

Jane glanced between him and the stereo, as if she was just putting together how hard the extra stimulus was for him. "Sure, of course. Ready to go?"

Theo nodded, though he still felt a bit shaky. Jane squeezed his arm, and the gesture brought some warmth back to him. He already started to forget the cold that had come over him.

Jane lowered the volume on the stereo. "You're just trying to avoid listening to me sing again, aren't you?"

Theo stared at her for a moment before he clicked that she was joking. "Well…" He played along and she gently shoved him.

They put on their seatbelts and drove back towards home.

*

The rest of the evening was relaxed. They cuddled up on the couch, ate their food, and watched a new Netflix film. Jane closed all her curtains so they were both certain that no one could see them.

Deep down, Theo still felt like Jack was up to no good – or would be – whether it was before or after Jane's field trip. Knowing that she would have to sleep a few tents away from him made Theo wrap his arms tighter around her. She didn't seem to notice.

The trip was only a few weeks away, but it felt closer every time he thought about it. Theo couldn't see into the future, but dread sat at the bottom of his stomach, Jane was completely oblivious to the way he felt.

24.

Jane

It was a week before the geography field trip. The days had passed quicker than Jane had expected. Her date with Theo had put them both on edge, and they hadn't gone out on another one. She didn't really feel up to it anyway. She didn't want to ruin everything before the year was over.

She felt like she was running to keep up with her busy life. Juggling schoolwork, applying for colleges, family, Theo, and hanging out with the group had her out of breath. Thankfully, with school finishing soon, her load would lessen.

During their second to last week of school before summer, Theo had become clingier. He tried to convince her not to go on the trip, but she had to considering it made up a big part of her final grade. Everyone would be there – Poppy and Nico included – so nothing bad would happen to her. Besides, the teachers would be in and out, checking on everyone throughout their time spent in the local woods.

She couldn't focus on that anyway. She had so many assignments to hand in that were taking up most of her brain power. Even though just last week they'd had their last tests, the teachers had thought it would be ok to give them more assignments, just to make their students' final grades look better.

Jane had been caught out a few times that week, while she was hanging out with the group. Jack would always throw a question her way when she wasn't concentrating. She'd end up flustered, trying to answer, which made everyone snicker at her. Her face would always burn red, but then again, she had mostly stopped caring what they thought of her. She was going to drop most of them soon, once summer started.

The second to last Friday before the summer break was pretty chill and she was grateful for that. Most of her teachers had let them just chat, work on their assignments, or play

170

games. Some even had a movie on. They knew better than to try and cram the last of the needed information into their student's brains, considering summer break started the next week.

Everyone was in a good mood too, which was nice. It was probably one of the only days Jane felt comfortable in school, just from the relief of it almost being over. She didn't even have to try to fit in. Now that she thought about it, most of the students probably felt the same. Everyone was just being themselves.

Walking home, she also felt lighter. She'd almost forgotten about the field trip. It hadn't even really crossed her mind, until Theo caught up. He thundered down on her rainbow, bringing her back to reality. It kind of annoyed her, but she couldn't blame him for being real. Someone had to be.

"Jane, what are you going to do about tomorrow?" He reached for her hand. They'd both started to feel more comfortable with their affection outside of their homes.

"It'll be ok," she said, trying to soothe his thoughts.

"How do we know that? I should come."

"You can't. Poppy and Nico will be there too, remember? It's a school trip."

"Yeah, I know, but Nico said Jack has been cooking something up."

Dread roiled in her stomach at that, but she tried to shrug it off. "It will be ok," she said again. "I'll message you if anything happens, alright?"

"But how am I meant to help if I'm back here?"

"We'll figure something out," Jane replied, giving him a hard stare.

They went inside. It was nice that Theo was being a protective boyfriend and all, but sometimes it was a bit much. She could tell he wanted to hover over her every move until she left tomorrow, but she needed to be alone. She made up an excuse that she needed to pack and make dinner.

Theo nodded but didn't seem to get that she wanted to do it by herself.

"Alone," she added.

His face fell but he shrugged, leaving solemnly, letting her have her peace.

She hadn't been lying when she said she had to pack and make some food for her mom. Her mom relied on Jane making sure she ate, so she would have to prepare food for all the nights she would be away.

Jane decided to make lasagna, which would last her mom the weekend. She expected to it be almost finished when she returned from her field trip. Jane prepared the layers, then placed it in the oven. She set the timer, then slipped upstairs to finish her packing while it cooked.

Half an hour later, Jane took the lasagna out of the oven. Her phone beeped – the sound of an email coming through on her school account. She put the lasagna to the side. Taking off her oven mitts, she picked up her phone off the kitchen benchtop. It was an email from her geography teacher.

Ms Williams,

Geography Research Field Trip,

Your group camping position has changed. You will now have to set up camp at the second entrance of the local woods. The second entrance is 3.5 miles further south. No need to worry, just thought I would spread out the groups more, so no one disrupts each other's research.

Walk through the wood entrance and you should see a little clearing where you'll be able to make camp.

See you tomorrow!

Jane shrugged to herself. To be honest, she hadn't paid much attention to where they were supposed to set up camp anyway, as she wasn't the one driving. She messaged Nico and Poppy. They'd both got the same email. At least they knew where they were going.

It did make sense to spread the groups out. A pleasant thought dawned on her. Hopefully this would mean she would be far, far away from Jack's tent.

*

About an hour later, the sun was still up in the sky. Jane loved summer, because of how long the day lasted.

Her mom appeared, ready to head off to work. She sat down with Jane and had a few bites of the lasagna, before packing some to take to work. After a few minutes of the usual chitchat, her mom excused herself.

She kissed Jane on the forehead. "Have a great trip tomorrow, love."

Jane watched as she disappeared through the front door. Once she was gone, silence echoed through the house, sending Jane into a trance.

Her phone rang from across the room, frightening her out of her daydream. Walking over, she picked it up. The caller profile showed up as Will.

"Hey!" she said.

"Are you crazy? Like seriously?"

Jane's eyebrows furrowed as she held her phone closer to her ear. She couldn't have heard that right.

"What?"

"Are you crazy, Jane?"

"What do you mean?"

"You can't seriously be this dumb?"

Jane took a step back, looking around in disbelief. Silence was the only answer she gave him.

Will sighed. "Sorry, I don't mean to sound angry, but Jane you can't go. He almost killed you."

"Go where?"

"Camping, Jane! Camping!"

Jane gasped. How did he find out? She hadn't told him because she knew he wouldn't want her to go.

"Did Theo tell you?!"

"How else would I know, Jane? He couldn't talk any sense into you."

"What! Ugh, how could he? It's a school field trip!"

173

"Theo is doing the sensible thing here! He has some sense in him." Will cleared his throat, and when he continued, his voice was quieter. "He's just looking out for you. Don't be angry at him."

Jane's anger was already dissipating. She knew why he'd done it. She was still annoyed about it though.

"Will, I'm going. It's for school. The teachers will be there."

"You know it's not smart right? Do you even need any more marks to pass?"

"No, but it'll make my grades look better. I've already agreed to go."

"Can't you back out?" Will's voice pleaded.

"Nope, and… and you can't change my mind." Jane was pleased with how firm her voice sounded.

He let out an exasperated sigh. Jane heard the resignation in it. He knew he couldn't do anything from wherever he was anyway.

"If anything happens, I…" Will trailed off, clearly not wanting to even think about it.

"Theo will sort it. It's ok. Jack's group isn't positioned close to ours. It'll be fine," Jane said.

Will sighed again, sounding too tired to fight anymore. "Well, just message or call so I know you're ok. Please?"

"Sure."

"Jane?"

"Yeah?"

"I'm sorry, and I love you."

"I love you too," Jane said. She listened to him breathing before ending the call. Jane really couldn't believe Theo told on her to her big brother. She guessed he felt like he had to, but she was still mad about it.

Jane wrapped her arms around herself and sat down on the couch. She'd never felt like anyone cared about her before. At least not in the way Theo did. She realized now how much Will cared too. She couldn't possibly stay mad at either of them. They were both just looking out for her.

She sent a message to Theo to come over, and he showed up in a matter of minutes. He stood outside her back door, looking like a child about to be told off.

Jane gestured for him to come in, and he silently opened her door and clicked it back in place. He tiptoed around her, ready for her wrath which never came.

She nodded to the couch, and he sat down next to her. He looked at her guiltily, not knowing that he was already forgiven. She moved closer to him and snuggled into his side.

Theo felt tense, as she placed her hand on his toned stomach. After a while, he relaxed, letting his arms close around her. There was no need for words. Soon after she felt him doze off, his strong arms gently around her still. Moving her head to look at his soft features, his chest fell and rose. He looked so at peace. Smiling, she thought to herself, *I really love this boy.*

## 25

Jane

Sun beamed into the lounge, striking both of them in the face. They had fallen asleep entwined together on the couch. Jane woke up to Theo looking down at her lovingly. He kissed her on the forehead and butterflies flared up inside her, making her feel all giddy. He pulled her closer to him, his arms now firmly wrapped around her again. They lay like this for a moment before Jane tried to pull away.

"You're not going anywhere!" he said cheekily.

"Let gooo." She jabbed her fingers into his side and his hands sprung open instantly. He squirmed away from her tickling hands.

She had him just where she wanted. She tickled him again, making him roar with laughter. Throwing his head back, he wriggled around. Theo edged closer and closer to the end of the couch.

Seeing what was about to happen, she quickly embraced him again as they fell off the couch together. He wrapped around her like a cocoon, taking most of the brunt once they hit the floor.

Theo rolled them over, hands on either side of her, and pulled himself up. Jane snapped her eyes open and looked up at him. The sun radiated behind him, giving him a halo. She was so in love with him. Both leaning into each other, they kissed. Warmth filled Jane. She couldn't help herself and raised her hands again to jabbed him in the sides. Instantly, his hands flew up protectively, and he fell on her. They both burst out laughing.

Wriggling out from underneath him, she stood, looking down at him. He had changed so much in the time she'd known him, and she couldn't be happier.

The front door creaked, and both she and Theo jerked their heads towards the noise.

Jane's mom slowly stepped inside, taking her time to fully enter. Theo jolted up and stood next to Jane. They watched her mom twist the doorknob as quietly as she could, making a soft clicking noise. Her mom exhaled a breath of relief and brushed her hands against one another. She patted her thighs and turned to go to the kitchen, halting. It was as if she rewound herself, turning back in their direction. There was a moment of awkward stares before they all burst into laughter.

"What were you doing, Mom?"

"I was trying to be quiet, because like you could've been sleeping in…?" She shrugged.

Jane gave her mom a warm hug. Her mom took a second to respond, then slowly hugged Jane back.

"I hear you drive up every time by the way, so don't worry about being quiet. But thanks."

"I was just trying," she replied, giggling.

They let go of each other.

"I need—"

"A shower," Jane finished for her mom, and they both laughed again.

Her mom said a quick hello to Theo and then headed upstairs to shower and sleep off her night shift.

Moving into the kitchen, Jane grabbed a frying pan and started to cook Theo some breakfast. He worked around her, grabbing plates and cutlery.

They sat at the breakfast bar, happily eating, until Jane's phone beeped. It was a text message from Poppy.

BE THERE IN AN HOUR, COMING IN NICO'S CAR. APPARENTLY JACK'S SITE GOT CHANGED TOO! CLOSER TO US…

Jane's stomach dropped so fast she almost regurgitated a piece of toast. Theo moved to her side instantly, reading the message.

"Your site got changed?" Theo asked.

"Yeah, last night."

"Where?"

"The second entrance."

"And Jack's did too? You don't have to do this," Theo said.

Jane smiled up at him, but she knew that she couldn't drop out now.

"It'll be ok, Theo," she said, stroking his arm.

He leaned down and kissed her shoulder, holding her for a moment.

"Let's go pack?" Jane asked. She'd mostly finished packing last night, but she could see Theo needed a distraction. She held his hand, as they made their way towards the stairs.

*

Around an hour later, they'd finished packing. It took longer than it should have, as Theo kept unpacking her things, stalling the process.

Jane grabbed her jacket, bringing it downstairs while Theo brought her backpack. Jane heard Nico's car pull up. She felt Theo's gaze on her back and turned around to kiss him. It was a heated and passionate kiss.

Theo handed over Jane's backpack, and she opened the door. Theo stepped out with her, waving towards Nico and Poppy. She gave his hand a quick squeeze before she walked down her steps and toward the car. She turned around. Theo's eyes were still on her.

Poppy hopped out of the car and gave Jane a quick hug. Poppy winked and glanced back toward the door, waving to Theo.

Jane put her bag in the trunk and hopped into the back seat. Poppy hopped in next to Nico. Jane let out a breath. Her nerves were bubbling.

"Hey Nico."

He met her eye in the rearview mirror and said hello back.

As Nico pulled away from her house, Jane looked back. Theo watched, his eyes following the car further and further down the road before they turned the corner. Poppy turned around and gave Jane a reassuring squeeze on her knee as she settled back into her seat.

*

The drive had been mostly uneventful and about forty-five minutes later, they arrived at the campsite. Finding the second entrance had been harder than they thought. They had driven past it twice before they saw it.

They were the first to arrive at the campsite. Her teacher messaged saying she would come around to the different sites to check on them at around 7 p.m. The clock had only just passed 6 p.m., Jane guessed that gave them more time to do research and set up.

They had just begun unpacking when another car showed up. Tommy was behind the wheel, Jack next to him, and Sam was in the back. Jack had a sinister smile plastered across his face which made Jane's skin crawl. She looked back to Nico and Poppy.

"I didn't think they were going to be this close to our campsite," Jane whispered.

"I didn't think so either," Poppy said. Nico just shrugged.

Jane quickly picked up her backpack out of the trunk and walked off into the woods, determined to put some distance between her and Jack. Poppy and Nico followed shortly afterwards. They found the clearing where they would be camping and went to work setting up.

Poppy and Jane's tent was up and they were helping with Nico's when the boys strolled over.

"Looks like Miss put us in the same spot..." Jack started.

Jane's heart dropped. She had her back to him and she really didn't want to turn around.

"Clearly that was a mistake," Nico said. He didn't even try to disguise the animosity in his voice.

Jane turned just as she saw Jack grin a stupid, sly smile. "Don't go getting mad at me. I didn't assign the spots."

Nico's jaw clenched. "Maybe you should go find somewhere else."

179

Jack raised his eyebrows. He looked to Tommy and Sam. "Dude thinks he's kicking us out."

Tommy and Sam snickered in response.

"Just get lost! None of us want you here." Nico stepped towards Jack, his anger visibly bubbling over.

Jane turned around. Fear gripped her. Nico was strong, but Jack fought dirty, and Tommy and Sam would back him up. She couldn't let Nico get hurt because of her.

Poppy stepped between them. "Nico, back off. They can just set up over there, so we don't disrupt each other's research," Poppy said, pointing to an area across from where they were.

"Yeah… good idea." Jack said. He picked up his bag and nodded to where Poppy pointed. He made his way over with Sam and Tommy following him.

Poppy turned to Jane. "It will be fine. We don't even have to talk to them." She glanced back at Nico. "Just try and stay calm, ok babe?"

They all continued with their camp set-up. Jane, Poppy, and Nico finished about ten minutes later and started their research project. They were writing about the environment around them when Jack interrupted. Their teacher was due to check in any minute now.

"Hey! Do you guys want takeout? We're going to go and get some soon."

"Nah, we're good." Nico spoke for them.

"Are you sure? We really don't mind."

"We have food," Nico said firmly. "Thanks, though," he added after a beat.

"I could just grab you guys some fries?" Jack was insistent. His eyes darted to Jane's. He seemed to be using all his power to hold back his frustration.

"Sure, we'll have some fries." Jane said. Anything to make him leave.

"Not even a pretty please with that? Wow," Jack said as he strolled away.

Jane couldn't be more thrilled that they were leaving, even if it was only for a bit. Her teacher should be here soon, so they could always ask to change spots while they were gone.

*

The teacher didn't show at 7 p.m. Nico muttered something about her maybe being stuck with another group, making her late, but Jane found it hard to believe. Something was bothering her.

She took out her phone and checked the email about the change of site. Didn't her teacher normally email from a school address? This had come from a Gmail one in the same name.

An uneasy feeling settled over Jane. The email, the boys being at the same site, and now the teacher not coming – things weren't adding up. Maybe her teacher didn't even know they were there? Maybe she thought they just decided not to turn up to the trip…

Jack, Sam, and Tommy arrived back with the food. The atmosphere between them seemed different. They were quiet and unsure of their movements as they walked over to them. Tension gripped Jane's chest. She exchanged a puzzled look with Poppy, but it was Nico who took the lead. He moved in front of the girls defensively.

"I thought it would be nice to all eat dinner together, don't you think?" Jack sat down followed by Sam and Tommy. Poppy lightly touched Nico's arm, trying to get him to relax. She sat down, pulling Nico down with her. Jane hesitated. She felt silly being the only one standing, but she couldn't quite stomach the idea of eating a meal with Jack. She sat down, hesitantly. Tommy and Sam tracked her movement. They couldn't seem to keep their eyes off her as they ate quietly.

"You guys seen the teacher? When we drove in, she was just walking to another group's campsite. She stopped us because she recognized our car. We almost got busted for leaving, but we gave her a burger. I think she continued on doing her checks, but she warned us not to leave again," Jack said which broke the awkwardness.

But why hadn't the teacher continued on her rounds to check on their group? Could she not find them? Jane bit into a fry, unwilling to voice the question.

Everyone kept shifting, trying to get comfortable, putting Jane more on edge. She reached into her pocket to take out her phone to message Theo, but it wasn't there. She must have left it in her tent. She went to get up when Jack's voice boomed out making them all jump.

"You've been lying to us Jane," Jack said suddenly.

Jane's stomach got caught in her throat. Silence echoed around them.

"Dude, you're being weird. Whatchu on about?" Nico chuckled, trying to turn the situation around.

"It's true, you've been ditching us for The Freak. I thought you were busy with assignments. You were cool until he came along." Sam said, backing up Jack.

If Jane could have disappeared in that moment, one hundred percent she would have. She straightened up, holding everything tense.

"Yeah, I wasn't so sure about it until the party," Tommy said. "And you two!" he said pointing to Nico and Poppy, "you two helping them! You don't know who your friends are, huh?" He finished off sourly.

Jane's eyes jumped from person to person. Sam and Tommy glared back at her. Why? Why were they so angry about this? All she'd done was hang out with a friend. What Jack had done was objectively so much worse, but none of them seemed to care about that.

Jane drew all her strength together. Poppy squeezed her hand.

"He's not a freak, he's just a little different, but you don't understand. And yes, I kept it a secret, but only because none of you wanted to give him a chance," she said. She felt her face fall into a pleading expression.

"Wrong answer, bitch," Jack barked.

Movement erupted from all angles. Sam and Tommy pounced on Nico. Poppy dropped Jane's hand and tried to free him. Nico said something unintelligible. Tommy left Sam to tumble with Nico after he got a few good hits in. He stalked toward Poppy. Panic crossed her face, as he wrapped his hands around her.

Jane, grabbing him, ripped his arm away from Poppy. Even in the heat of the moment, Jane could see Jack watching, waiting to step in at the right moment.

Nico broke free, dashing toward Poppy. His fist smashed into Tommy's face. Tommy stumbled backwards, and then Sam was back on him.

Jane's head spun. She heard Jack shouting for Tommy to get back up.

Jane pushed Poppy behind her. Her friend's tear-streaked face was childlike, and Jane felt a surge of protective instinct.

Jack and Tommy laughed, closing in on them. Tommy walked over to his campsite and grabbed some rope. Sam had forced Nico to the ground, squishing his face into the dirt.

Nico looked towards Poppy, terror crossing his face. Tommy bent down, and helped Sam tie him up. Jane held out her hands, still desperately trying to protect Poppy, and backed further and further away. Poppy hit a tree and laid her hands on Jane's back, gesturing for her to stop.

Jane looked around for anything she could use as a weapon. She spotted a stick and snatched it up, pointing it like a dagger.

"Aw, how cute," Jack said, pulling a puppy dog face.

Tommy darted forward. Jane smacked him across the face with her stick. He froze, startled by the hit. The three of them stared at one another, surprised Jane had struck him.

Then Tommy grinned, and moved closer, grabbing the stick from her. Panic flew through Jane as he pulled it forward, grabbing her with it. She tried to push him off which made him laugh.

"No!" Poppy dove forward, reaching for Jane.

Jack caught her around the waist, hoisting her up. He walked her back towards Nico. She thrashed and screamed as he put her down next to Nico whose face had started to change color. Holding her wrists together, Jack tied them and then her ankles.

"Let me go!" Poppy kicked out as hard as she could. Jack grabbed her and slapped her across the face. The strike echoed around the campsite. Everyone froze, staring at Jack. Poppy whimpered, then fell quiet.

Nico pushed himself up, trying to drag himself over to her. Jack pushed Nico's face into the dirt again with his foot.

"This wouldn't have had to happen if you two weren't so weak. Just stay still and stay out of way. We'll deal with you later," Jack shouted.

Poppy whimpered again and shuffled over toward Nico. Jack took his foot off Nico's head and Nico scrambled, moving to Poppy. She raised her bound hands, cupping his face and rubbing away at the dirt.

Everyone's attention turned back to Jane. Tommy tightened his grip on her. Sweat broke out on her forehead. She felt Tommy look down at her, and she took her chance. She whipped her head back, smashing the back of her skull against his nose. He reared back, clutching his face.

Jane scrambled away, but Jack lunged at her, forcing her to the ground.

His knees pinned her hips, and the rest of his weight held down her arms. Jane kicked but got nowhere. His eyes filled with determination.

Jane should have listened to Theo. How could she have been so, so wrong? Suddenly the fight went out of her.

"That's better. Just give up. Your freak isn't here to help you." Jack's words wrapped around her throat.

"Why are you doing this?!" Jane spat in his face.

He wiped his cheek on his sleeve and turned back to Jane. Her blood turned cold, as he leaned in, his face just a few inches from hers.

"Ever since he came to our school you have been obsessed with him. Not me! Him! But I have a special surprise for you to help with that!" he said giddily. He was insane.

"You're a psychopath!"

"You always think you're above us don't you, Jane? Not for much longer." He pinned her arms with one hand, cupping her chin with the other.

"Let me go!"

"Oh, hush. Don't be silly." He spoke like Jane was a naughty child to be placated. "You know, I think we just need to get to know each other better. I'm thinking something more… intimate."

The blood drained from Jane's head, and she felt like she was going to pass out. She started thrashing again, trying to free herself.

Jack pressed down on her, his whole weight crushing the air from her lungs. A sob escaped her lips, and Jack grinned, malice dripping from him.

"Please… you can't. You wouldn't do that." Jane felt everyone's eyes on her.

"You mean, wouldn't we?" He looked at Sam and Tommy.

"You're sick! Let her go!" Nico yelled.

Jack rolled his eyes and pointed back at him. Someone moved to the left and Jane heard a thrashing noise. After a few moments, muffled screams started, and she suspected Nico had been gagged.

Jack's attention turned back to Jane. His hand slid down her face and neck, over her collar bone, and down to her stomach. She started to shake as his hand got closer to her shorts. She looked around desperately.

His hand slithered further. He adjusted himself, giving Jane a tiny glimmer of hope. Forcing her knee up, she hit him right in the bullseye. He doubled over in pain.

Jane shoved him off and stood up. For a moment she couldn't move, the horror of the whole night froze her in place. And then Poppy's voice rang out.

"Jane! RUN!"

26.

Jane

Present,

Jane's eyes snap open. A tingling sensation crosses her cheek, intensifying as she wakes up. The moon shines through the undergrowth, giving her a little light.

The sensation crawls up towards her nose and over to her other cheek. Drawing her lips into a thin line, she moves cautiously into a spot of light. She takes a deep breath and looks down. Instead of seeing her nose, all she sees is a big furry spider.

Her eyes widen with fear, bullets of sweat start forming on her skin. Watching it move towards her lips, each leg feels like its Velcroed to her face, lifting her skin slightly before ripping off.

The spider continues to makes its way down to her lips. Blinking back tears, Jane reaches out to grab… anything. Grasping a leaf, she carefully puts it in front of the spider. The creature cautiously walks onto it, taking its time. It feels like it takes a lifetime for the spider to climb completely onto the leaf. Jane gingerly lifts it away from her face and throws it into the bush.

As soon as it's gone, Jane sits upright. The blood rushes from her head, making her dizzy and disorientated. She lets out the scream she's been holding in, then smacks her hands over her mouth.

She can't let Jack hear her.

She looks down at her leg, her hands still covering her mouth. She almost faints again; her ankle is ruined!

Her breaths quicken, and she can feel herself starting to hyperventilate. How can she get away if she can't even walk?

A thought strikes her, and she takes a big gulp of air. Are Poppy and Nico still trapped at the campsite? She has to get out of here, for them, not just herself.

Jane reaches into her pocket hoping for her phone. She remembers that she left it in her tent.

She can hear distant laughter and voices – Jack, Sam, and Tommy. Nausea rolls in her stomach, and she feels like she's going to puke. She'd rather be anywhere else but near them.

Reaching down towards her foot, she gently touches her ankle. It's already swollen up to the size of a tennis ball.

Careful not to make too much noise, she feels around for something she could use as a splint. A couple of sticks are the best she comes up with.

She slides her foot from her shoe and excruciating pain shoots up the length of her leg. The idea of straightening it makes her stomach turn when it already hurts this much. She takes a moment just to breathe, then pulls the laces from her shoes, planning to use them to hold the makeshift splint in place.

"Please let this work," she whispers to herself. She has no idea whether it will, but it's her only hope.

Finding another stick, she places it in her mouth. That was what they did in movies, wasn't it? She hopes biting down on it will stop her making too much noise.

Gingerly, she places her hands on either side of her foot. She takes a deep breath, then wrenches hard, yanking her ankle back into the right position.

Pain burns through her, and she falls back trembling. She keeps biting down on the stick, no longer feeling the need to scream. Boiling tears rush down her cheeks, as she lets out a few pained moans.

Rolling her hands into fists, she pushes herself back up, looking down at her now semi-normal ankle. She puts the splint in place by resting a thick stick on either side of her ankle and tying the shoelaces tightly around.

She has never felt this much pain before in her life. Working as fast as she can, she finishes the makeshift splint. She spits out the stick and looks down at the job she's done. It's not perfect, but it will go some way to mobilizing her joint again.

Out of breath, she fixates her eyes on the moon above her, trying to steady her heartbeat.

*

Theo

Five hours earlier,

Watching Jane walk out to the car, knowing that Jack was going to be on the same school trip, had made Theo sick to his stomach. He left shortly after he saw the car drive around the corner. He made sure everything was locked up and in its place, and even put a load of washing on for Jane's mom before walking out the back door, across Jane's yard and into his own.

Inside, his mom was baking, kneading dough on the countertop. She had flour on the tip of her nose and all over her shirt. Theo chuckled, but when he looked back at her face, she looked worried.

"What's wrong, Mom?"

She turned back around, wiping her hands on her backside. She opened the medicine cabinet. Theo watched her sift through the cupboard contents, mumbling for him to stay put. He did what he was told, staring down at the half-finished baking. He caught sight of his reflection in the stainless-steel bowl, and his mother's behavior suddenly made sense.

He was as pale as newly fallen snow. He touched his face, noticing it was slick with sweat. His hands were shaking too – an all too familiar feeling. Was he sick? Or was it the stress catching up with him?

His mom turned back around with a thermometer and shoved it into Theo's mouth. She rested her palm on his forehead, even though it was sticky with perspiration. The thermometer beeped, and she took it out of his mouth, gazing at it.

"Honey, you have a fever. A high one. Sit down, sit down." Pulling out a chair, she ushered Theo into it. "Do you feel sick? You're burning up!"

"Whoa Mom, calm down. I don't feel sick. I just feel cold and sweaty. I think I'll go have a shower. It's ok." Theo stood.

"Are you sure?"

"Yes. I'll call you if I feel worse. I think it's just overdue stress from school assignments."

His mom stared at him, concern creasing her forehead. "Well … as long as you tell me if you feel worse, ok?"

"Sure, Mom."

His mom moved forward, embracing him. Theo's arms easily rested around her shoulders, and he sunk into her, forgetting how long it had been since they'd hugged. She looked up at him, her expression hard to read, before letting go and continuing with her dough.

Theo passed his dad napping on the couch. He looked tired. His hair was completely gone now, but the colors in his face were starting to return to normal. For a while he'd taken on a reddish complexion because of the radiation treatment. Thankfully the radiation seemed to work in his favor. He was now on his last weeks of chemotherapy to get rid of the final cancer cells.

If Theo could sum his dad up as anything right now, it was a picture of hope.

Theo took the stairs two at a time, grabbing some spare clothes and a towel once he was in his room. He checked his phone and sent a quick message to Jane, hoping there would be a reply by the time he got out of the shower. He set his phone down on the bathroom counter and turned on the water.

*

Theo's phone still hadn't beeped. Annoyance had turned to concern, then straight to fear. His head rumbled with worry, making him dizzy.

His mum called him down for dinner and throughout the whole meal, Theo tried to hide his dizziness. His mother's eyes were continually on him and once they finished she gave him a glass of water and some Tylenol and told him to go to bed early.

Present,

Theo sat on the edge of his bed again, holding his phone. His anxiety rises and falls with every breath he takes. Something didn't feel right, and his mind couldn't settle.

He stands, pacing back and forth. A cold feeling overtakes him, the same feeling he experienced when he and Jane went out on their date. Anxious butterflies seize control of his stomach, churning it.

Theo changes into some sweatpants and a hoodie, then slips his running shoes on. He wouldn't be able to sleep if he couldn't calm himself down.

Grabbing his headphones, Theo walks down the stairs, sending a quick message to his mom, telling her that he's going for a run.

He hears a chair scrape over the floorboards, then her footsteps making their way across the room. Theo opens the front door before she can reach him, stepping out into the night.

A warm wind hits Theo as he steps off the porch. He walks to the first streetlamp before breaking into a jog. He hears a door behind him close softly, most likely his mom watching him run down the street.

His phone buzzes in his pocket. Excitement and hope rise inside him as he pulls it out. But it's just a message from his mom, nothing from Jane. His shoulders drop.

"Screw it," he says aloud. He calls Jane, hoping she will pick up.

Five rings in and his anxiety is building again. Of course she won't pick up. She's having a blast without him no doubt.

Suddenly the phone clicks, the ring cutting out. He slows his run, listening, but all he can hear is static.

"Hello? Jane?"

"Theo?!" someone asks in a trembling voice.

"Who is this? Where's Jane?"

"I don't know where she is. She ran into the woods and he won't wake up. They won't let us out and… and…" the girl trails off, bursting into sobs.

Theo's blood runs cold as he realizes who it is. "Poppy? Who won't wake up?"

"Nico! They kept hitting him and hitting him and when I told Jane to run, that was the end of it."

"Shh, shh, ok? It's going to be ok." Panic rattles through Theo, every muscle in his body tensing. "I'm coming to get you and we are going to find Jane. Poppy? I need you to stay calm for me, ok?"

Poppy whimpers. "Ok, but be careful."

"See you soon."

In the background, Theo hears voices coming closer. Suddenly the line goes dead. Theo stares at the now blank phone, determination now running through him.

Turning around, he races back to the house. He slips inside quietly and grabs his mom's car keys from the hook by the door.

He climbs into his mom's car, starting it up. The lights turn on upstairs, and his mom's horrified face stares out at him, through the curtain.

"What do you think you're doing, Theo?!" she yells.

Theo reverses out of the driveway. He rolls down the passenger window and leans over the center console. "They need me," he yells. "She needs me! Call the police or something! Tell them it's Jack at the local woods where you can camp."

His mom's face is a mask of hurt and confusion, but Theo doesn't stop. He puts the car into drive and takes off down the street.

## 27

## Jane

When Jane's heartbeat has steadied, she moves her gaze from the moon to a tree stump nearby. If she can just drag herself over, she'll be able use it to get to her feet. Her pulse throbs in her ankle, like a second heartbeat. She scoots herself backwards on her rear until she reaches the stump.

Pain shudders through her, and she has to stop. She takes several big breaths, forcing herself to hold each to get control.

She gets her good leg under her, and she presses up with her hands using all her remaining strength. For a moment, she thinks she's going to come crashing back down, but the stump is there for support.

Brushing the dirt off her hands, she looks down at her foot. Blood rushes down to it, the color coming back, as pins and needles stab her. She's just thankful that she can still feel something down there. The fear of severed blood vessels and tendons had been on her mind as she forced her ankle back into place.

Jane looks up at the hill she tumbled down, squinting. The left side seems like her best option – it has decent grooves cut out of it, which she could use as stairs. She leans down, searching for a long stick to help her balance. The best she finds is an old branch with leaves still attached. It will have to do.

Grunting, she pulls herself upright, tentatively putting some weight on her injured ankle. Regret rushes through her bones, warning signals firing through her body. She takes the weight off her ankle just as fast as she can.

Taking a seat again she sighs. Focus on Poppy, focus on Nico, she thinks to herself. She has to help her friends.

She tries again, this time using the stick to support her weight. This is better. She takes a step, then another. It hurts, but it's bearable this time. A few more steps, and she has some sort of motion going and slowly makes her way over to the side of the hill.

Already she can hear voices from the campsite. She bites her tongue, vowing not to make a sound while climbing up. She hopes to drag herself back to the campsite without being seen. She needs to reach her phone; hopefully there'll be enough coverage. She has to call for help, or they're all screwed.

Using her hands and her one good leg, she hauls herself further and further up the hill. She uses her knee like an anchor on the other side.

The process is frustratingly slow, and she has to stop for many breaks. Finally, she reaches the top.

Her hand flails about, trying to find anything to pull herself up. Her fingers curl around the long, stringy leaves of a flax bush. She clings to them, fists clasping handfuls, nearly yanking the bush from the ground as she pulls herself up onto the hilltop. Letting go of the bush, she lays back, resting her hands on her stomach, breathing hard.

"Did anyone else hear something, or am I going crazy?"

Jane's head snaps up at Tommy's voice. She looks to her side, only now noticing she is out in the open. Dread fills her, and in a rush, she rolls over, disappearing into the bushes.

Her feet get tangled in the undergrowth, but she tugs them free, sending a stab of pain up her leg.

A pained yelp escapes her lips. She claps a hand over her mouth, biting down on it. Her other hand grabs her leg, yanking it back into the bushes.

A rush of footsteps circle her, hushed voices following them. They were getting closer to where she was hiding. Suddenly, a bird flew out from the bush across the clearing.

"Tommy, are you serious? Just chill, it's a friggin bird" Jack says. He twists around and heads back to where they were sitting. Sam follows after him, but Tommy doesn't seem so sure. He glances out into the woods, double checking. Jane's head pounds from holding her breath. Eventually, he

too turns around and follows the others back to where the tents are set up.

Jane doesn't move, waiting for everything to quiet down. Finally, there is silence, but still Jane waits, wanting to be sure. She makes her way closer to the camp. Every sound seems amplified. She places her feet carefully, but leaves rustle and twigs snap under her weight. Each time she stops, she freezes, dreading the sound of Jack coming for her.

Jane finally drags herself around to the back of her tent. Pressing up against it she reaches for the zipper, hoping to be able to slip her hand in and grab her phone out of her bag. Movement inside the tent makes her freeze once more. Her blood turns to ice, and everything seems to slow down. She has to get as far away as she can, before they realize she's there. Trying to creep away from the tent she hears the zipper on the other side tug down, little by little. It's too late to run.

Poppy's face appears in the gap. Relief floods through Jane, but she raises her finger to her lips.

Poppy's face flips through a range of emotions, as she stays mercifully quiet. She turns her back, grabs the zipper again between her bound hands, inching it down further.

Jane shuffles back to the tent and slides inside the small opening, awkwardly negotiating her busted ankle through it.

She knows she must look awful, but her relief at seeing Poppy overshadows everything else. Poppy closes the zipper behind Jane and takes a seat. They stare at each other, too scared to make a noise.

Jane looks down at Nico. He's still tied up and slumped on the floor. Asleep or unconscious? Jane couldn't tell.

"I'm going to untie you," Jane tells Poppy in a low whisper, "but if someone comes, you need to act like you're still tied up and asleep, ok?" Jane doesn't know what she will do if someone comes. There's nowhere to hide in here.

Poppy nods, still too afraid to speak. Digging through both their bags, Jane finally finds a small knife.

Poppy's eyes widen when she sees it, but she turns her back, and holds out her hands for Jane to free. It takes forever, the back-and-forth motion of the knife damaging Jane's hands more than it does the rope. But slowly… slowly… it starts to wear.

Finally, Poppy's hands spring apart. Once she's free, her first reaction is to grab Jane. "I thought you were dead!" she hisses, tears streaming down her face.

"Shhh…" Jane hisses back as she returns the hug. "Can you untie your legs?"

Poppy nods, and Jane turns to Nico's hands. Gently, Jane cuts his wrists free, letting them drop either side of him. She and Poppy work on freeing his legs. They spring apart too, once released, but the movement is short-lived. He's definitely unconscious, Jane thinks, as they both study his bruised face.

"Where's my phone?" Jane asks Poppy.

Poppy pulls the phone from underneath her.

"Jack heard me talking to Theo earlier, so I gave him mine. I've been sitting on yours this whole time, hoping I could get free to use it."

"You called Theo?"

"He was calling you, I just managed to answer it. I tried to call for help, but I couldn't dial with my hands behind me."

"You did great," Jane says.

Poppy shifts, her limbs clearly sore from having been bound for so long, and her hand comes down on Jane's ankle.

Jane screams. "Get off, get off!"

Poppy draws back her hand, clapping it over Jane's mouth to muffle her cries. Shock fills her face, as she gazes down at Jane's ankle.

A wave of dizziness comes over Jane, but she shakes it off, along with Poppy's hand.

"Quick! Tie Nico up again, so he still can escape, and wrap the rope around you. Tell them you had a nightmare," Jane says in a hushed, panicked voice.

Everyone would have heard her that time. Poppy does what she's told, and Jane wraps the rope loosely around her wrists.

"Fake sleep. Hurry, they're coming! If he finds me, do nothing. You never saw me."

"But—"

"No Poppy. I'll be ok."

Muffling her cries, Poppy lies down and huddles into Nico, who's starting to show signs of consciousness. Jane grabs the phone and starts unzipping the back of the tent. She disappears into the bushes, just as someone reaches the tent, ripping open the front zipper.

Jane keeps moving, despite the pain. Behind her, she can hear Jack and Tommy searching the tent. Both Poppy and Nico mumble something as if they had just been woken up.

She dials the police as she limps, and the receiver picks up. Trying to manoeuvre with a phone to your ear and only one good leg was harder than she thought. She was trying to get as far away from the camp as she could before they found her.

She pauses, now a safe enough distance away to crouch down and hopefully still out of sight.

"Do you need police, ambulance, or fire?"

"Police," she whispers. The line clicks as she is put through to the police department.

"This is the police department, tell me exactly where you are and your situation."

"We are at the second entrance of the local woods, and he's gone crazy. He attacked me and my friends. He has them captured in a tent and I can't save them. Please help."

"The police are on their way. This emergency has been reported by someone else already. Stay where you are. They will be there soon. If you need this line again, call back." The receiver hangs up on her. She looks down at her phone in disbelief. Surely they should have stayed on the phone with her? Surely they didn't think they were getting a prank call?

She dials Theo's number. He picks up one ring in.

"Jane?!

"I'm here."

"Are you ok? Are you safe?"

Breathing hard, Jane ignores Theo's questions. It's gone quiet in the tent. She backs herself further away, into a hollow tree trunk, where she can still see the camp.

"Jane's not there," someone shouts.

Torches light up around the camp but they're searching the tents, not the woods. Jane lets out a big breath. She brings the phone back up her ear. "It's ok, Theo calm down. Just come get me, ok? I need you," she says.

"You need him, huh?" Jack appears out of the shadows.

Jane's blood turns cold. Her heart drops and her throat goes dry. She hears Theo scream down the line. Jack drops down to a crouching position. He reaches out, his hand cupping her face.

"It's nice to finally have you join us again," he says in a low, sinister voice.

His other hand rests on her ankle and slowly, he starts squeezing it. Agonizing pain scores through her.

"Stop! Please Jack, it hurts!"

Jack squeezed harder. Jane felt her body fall in on itself, crumpling like a puppet released from its strings.

28.

Theo

"Jane! JANE, ANSWER ME! I SWEAR IF YOU TOUCH HER, JACK—" The line goes dead. He can no longer hear Jane.

His blood boils and his foot gets heavy, pressing further down on the gas pedal. Five minutes from the local woods, panic rises inside him as he thinks about her pleading voice. He can't help but imagine the worse.

He slows down near the second entrance. The cars in the parking lot are familiar. He turns off his lights and rolls into a park beside them – on the end, positioned for a quick getaway.

Silently he gets out and closes the door behind him. He checks the trunk, hoping for something he can defend himself with. The best he comes up with is an umbrella.

Sighing, he closes the boot, umbrella in hand, and sets off down the path. Up ahead, there are lights and voices that sounded dreadfully familiar.

*

Jane

Jane wakes. She licks her dry lips, tasting blood in her mouth. She swallows it down. Above her, the tent roof looms. Jack's tent roof. Her hands are bound, but thankfully her feet are free. The pain in her ankle shoots up her leg like a lightning strike, making her feel lightheaded.

Hushed voices whisper outside the tent's entrance. They sound like they're trying to reason with Jack… thankfully the others had started to understand this has gone too far. Jack isn't having any of it. His voice rises in anger. Tommy and Sam's voices rise too, loud enough for Jane to hear.

199

"You can't do that, dude. It's gone too far! Did you see her ankle?" It sounds like Sam.

"Don't be such a wimp," Jack replies. "She deserves it. Anyway, it'll be fun."

"Yeah Sam. You don't have to." Tommy's voice this time.

"I just… I think we have done enough. Like seriously – we've gone too far," Sam says again. "We could all get arrested for this."

"Leave then! Or go to your tent. You don't have to be a part of this," Tommy says.

"Screw this, I'm getting out of here." Sam's footsteps pound away.

Jane bites her lip. For a moment she thought Sam might have been her lifeline. It's just Jack and Tommy now. Even though only Sam has left, it gives Jane a little bit of hope. Escaping might be easier now that all three aren't after her.

A tug at the tent's zipper makes Jane freeze. Her heart rate increases with every movement. She closes her eyes, forcing herself to lie still… to play dead, or at least unconscious.

She feels a body move roughly into the tent, zipping it back up behind them. He moves closer, and she can feel his eyes hover over her body. He places his hand gently on her thigh, letting it slide up her body.

"If you had just listened," Jack says softly, "this never would have happened. I'm a very proactive person, Jane. You're special… You're not like anyone else I know. I have to have you. I'm sorry it has to be like this."

Jane doesn't move. Does he think she's unconscious? Would he be saying any of this if he knew she could hear him?

He lets his hand slide further up. Jane wants to gag, to shudder and cringe away, but she forces herself to lie still. His cold hand makes contact just under her shirt. Goosebumps flush over her. He lifts his hand, breaking contact with her skin.

His palm now rests on her face, moving it towards him. He leans down, kissing her softly.

He rises from the kiss, and she feels his eyes on her face. He kisses her again, harder, tugging at her lips, as if trying to force a response from her.

Jack's no longer gentle with her, kissing her with agitation. Jane keeps still, though she wants to shove him away.

She feels him move away from her before returning, his weight on top of her now. She hears his zipper, the sound she's been dreading. But she won't let this happen without a fight. She exhales heavily before opening her eyes.

Her hands still bound she squeezes them together, punching upwards as hard as she can. She connects with his gut, winding him. He falls back, gasping for air.

"Help! Help me!" she screams.

She reaches for the tent wall, scrambling for the back entrance. There's no zipper. No way out. Jack recovers and picks up a torch, hurling it at her. She screams and blocks the blow with her bound hands. He grabs her again, by the hands, pulling her forward. She falls, screaming as her ankle twists. He claps his hand over her mouth, his weight coming down on her. Tears stream from her eyes.

The tent's zipper rips open, moonlight bursting in. Someone grabs him around the middle and throws him to the side. A second pair of hands come under Jane's arms and yank her up and out of the tent.

Poppy stares down at her.

"Run, Poppy! Just run!" Nico's voice comes from inside the tent.

They do. Poppy drags Jane. They make it to the trees and crouch down, hiding.

Jane's eyes flit around the campsite. She can't see Sam. Tommy lies to the side, clutching his stomach. He looks like he's unable to move from the pain of whatever blow Nico inflicted.

Jack and Nico are still inside the tent.

Poppy whimpers. "Nico told me to grab you and run…" She hesitates and then shakes her head. "But I can't leave him." Her words are barely a whisper.

"Help me get up." Jane holds out her bound hands. "We won't leave him."

Poppy undoes the rope. Shouts come from inside the tent, a pained scream from Nico.

"Find a stick," Jane says. "As big as you can."

Poppy nods and runs off, scanning the ground for a weapon.

Nico has stopped screaming, but thud after thud tells Jane Jack hasn't left him alone.

"Jack!" she yells. "JACK, STOP! PLEASE YOU'LL KILL HIM!"

She's not sure Jack will care. "STOP! PLEASE! KILL ME INSTEAD!"

She hears Jack laugh and then one more heavy thud. As Jack emerges from the tent, everything seems to be moving in slow motion. Nico's hand follows, grabbing at his leg, trying to hold him back. Jack kicks him and Nico's groan echoes through the camp.

Jack moves towards her, looking tired suddenly. Jane wants to look for Poppy, to pray she has found a stick, but she can't look away from Jack.

She backs away, hitting a tree behind her. There's nowhere else to go, and she can't run anyway. This is it. She wishes her last moment could have looked different, to mean something. Jack approaches, slowly. Jane's breath catches. She closes her eyes.

Nothing happens.

She waits, bracing for a blow. But there's nothing. No blow to the head. No hand around the throat. Nothing. Is she already dead?

Gingerly, she opens her eyes.

"Theo," she whispers.

Theo

"KILL ME INSTEAD!" Theo hears Jane scream.

An imaginary knife plunges into his abdomen, and he comes to a halt. Her voice. Her words replay over and over, and now the knife twists, slicing a groan out of him.

Just ahead of him, the rush of movement stops. Everything feels like it's in slow motion, as he watches Jack walk up to her. She wobbles back, hitting a tree. He's not going to make it in time. Adrenaline fuels him, and he surges forward.

He raises the umbrella and whacks Jack across the back of the head. He hears Jane utter his name. He tosses the umbrella aside and stands over Jack.

Anger takes over him. He grabs a handful of his shirt, lifting him and throwing punch after punch. Theo's vision blurs and rage pulses through his veins.

Someone moves to his side, gently touching his shoulder and tries to pull him back. He drops Jack with a thump. Blood splatters across his face. Breathless, Theo takes a step back. Blood coats every crevice of his hands. Looking up, guilt fills him, as he stares at everyone's frightened faces. No one dared to stop him except Jane.

Twisting around, Theo looks at her. Her clothes are a complete mess, half ripped, and dirt cakes almost every part of her bare skin. Her face is as pale as a piece of paper with splotches of yellow and purple showing. Her cracked lips part, trying to say Theo's name, failing at the first syllable. She bursts into tears.

Theo envelops her, becoming a human cocoon; his butterfly is finally safe within his walls. Jane's grip becomes stronger, which tells Theo that she is finally with him – body, brain, and soul.

His hands move up to her face, holding either side of it, just looking at her. Her fingers rest gently on his, their foreheads press together.

Laughter comes from behind them. Theo stands in front of Jane, still gripping her hand behind his back. A shield goes up inside him.

Jack slowly sits up, spitting out blood between breaths and his sickly laugh. He lets it echo throughout the woods, no one saying a word. "Bravo, bravo, The Freak finally became a MAN! I am surprised Theo, you won this time." He spits at them.

"If you ever, EVER lay a hand on her or anyone else again, you'll be dead," Theo says, through gritted teeth.

Jack bursts into a painful fit of laughter. It takes him a few minutes to catch his breath. Nico makes his way over to them, planting himself next to Theo. Sam watches from his tent and Tommy sits up, holding his middle, still out of breath. Nico looks worse for wear. Theo wonders how he will ever repay him.

Jack looks around at Sam and Tommy, raising his hands as if he's a Spartan leader. "Really? You're going to abandon me just like that? Some friends you are. And you're going to follow The Freak now?"

"You're the freak, Jack. You always have been," Nico says.

Jack casts a death stare at Nico. "Me? ME the freak?! You've got to be joking. I'm the only—"

Poppy pushes through the group and swings a stick, hitting him right in the face. He drops like a ton of bricks, finally blacking out.

"SHUT UP!" Poppy screams at him. She drops the stick and rushes into Nico's open arms. She wraps herself around him, taking some of his weight on her shoulders.

Theo's eyes jump between Sam and Tommy. Their faces are tired and worn, but their eyes seem to regain some sort of freedom. They both back away, moving to their tents, no doubt to pack up and head home. Or to sleep a few hours until the sun comes up.

Theo looks at the little group around him, all strong in their different ways. They slowly walk towards the parking lot,

Poppy helping Nico, and Theo supporting Jane. Theo can tell they all just want to get as far from the campsite as possible.

Theo glances back, checking Jack is still lying on the ground.

Jane goes limp. Instinctively, Theo's other arm wraps around her, taking all her weight. Her head falls back, and her breathing slows. A new type of panic grips at him, slapping at him with its reins.

He picks her up. "Open the car, Poppy!" He throws her the keys and she unlocks it, opening both passenger doors. Jane's lifeless body flops against him and Theo starts to run with her.

Nico falls into the passenger seat as Theo reaches them.

"What happened?!" Poppy helps get her into the back seat.

"I don't know, she just fainted." Theo closes the door and they both run to the other side of the car.

Lifting Jane's head, Theo rests it into his lap. Poppy jumps in the front and twists the ignition. The car roars to life. Shifting it into reverse, she puts her foot down. She races out of the gates, then swings them around. Nico and Theo hold on for dear life as she puts it into drive and they sprint off again.

Nico and Theo exchange petrified looks, but Poppy focuses on the road ahead. She puts her seatbelt on, one-handed.

"You are never driving again," Nico mutters which she ignores.

Theo glances between them, and then down at Jane whose eyes start to twitch. "Theo?" Her voice is weak.

"I'm here. You've got to stay awake for me, ok?"

She grabs Theo's hand and lifts it to her mouth. He can feel her smile against his fingertips before she softly kisses them. Still holding his hand, she looks up at him. "I love you."

His heart jumps into his throat. Warmth spreads throughout him, and he realizes at that very moment he wants to be with her forever. Tears spill out as an overwhelming amount of love for her rushes through him.

"I love you too and I'm never letting you go again."

She raises her hand to wipe away his tears. Theo kisses her fingertips.

He glances out the front window, hoping to see the lights of town. Darkness surrounds them and they're still half an hour or so away from home, depending on how much Poppy is willing to break the speed limit. Two police cars race past them, going towards the campsite, their flashing lights illuminating the darkness. They didn't seem to notice Poppy speeding.

Jane's hand goes heavy in Theos. It falls from his grip, along with all his hopes.

Terror seizes him as he looks down at her. Her skin has taken on the look of a newly painted China doll, her lips so pale they're barely visible... "Shit, shit, shit, shit!"

"What? What is it, dude?" Nico turns pale as he looks down at Jane. "Poppy, hurry up!" he yells.

Not needing to be told twice, Poppy puts her foot down all the way. The revs count up, as the engine works harder than it ever has before. Theo searches Jane's neck for a pulse. It's weak. He starts to cry again.

"Jane? Jane?! Wake up? Please, please, it's ok now. I've got you. Wake up for me, please?" He brushes her hair out of her face, moving from his seat to lean over her. He rests his head lightly on her chest, feeling for her breaths. They slow with every exhale. He grips her face in his hands, his voice raw, "Wake up! Jane, wake up, please! Jane!"

## 30

## Theo

Reds and blues; emergency colors light up the car. They're the only thing that can help Jane right now. Poppy got them there really fast.

They all brace for a speed bump coming up. The car flies over it and the back shocks give way, slamming the trunk into the concrete.

Poppy speeds around the emergency department's parking lot before slamming on the brakes. Theo struggles to hold Jane on the seat as he hits the back of the front seats. Nico grips him, stopping him from flying forward through the windscreen.

Theo opens the car door and hoists Jane up. Her life seeps out from under her. Theo grips her tighter, trying to force some of it to stay inside, but it's not enough.

The shock hits Poppy as she gets out of the car, and a shrill wail breaks through her lips. She falls to the ground and Nico huddles over her, rocking them both back and forward. Fear grips Theo and he takes a stumbling step forward before breaking into a full run.

He turns, pushing the door open with his back. Shocked faces greet him. Everything seems to slow down as he pushes his way to the front desk, parting a sea of people.

"Please help. You gotta help her. I don't know if she's breathing. I don't—" A gurney hits the back of his legs. Breathless, he places Jane on it and the nurses and doctors huddle around her. Still gripping her hand, he's pulled along with them to the ER.

They cut her top. Someone listens for her heartbeat. They cover her with sticky things.

A dizzy wave of concern crashes over Theo. His eyes fixate on her hand as they place it back on the bed. He's being pushed further and further away.

Her hand jolts up and falls back to the bed again, lifeless. Theo is outside the doors now. Someone says something but Theo can't understand the words. Her hand is in the air again, holding there for a millisecond.

Theo falls against the wall. He slides to the floor, arms and legs curling up, and begins rocking, rocking, rocking.

He didn't make it in time. He never should have let her go. He should have been there. But he wasn't. He wasn't. He wasn't.

He wasn't there when she needed him the most, and now Jane is paying the price. Hot anger burns through him as he huddles into himself, not realizing another pair of hands have surrounded him, holding him tight.

*

Theo looks up after who knows how long. Light blinds him, his eyes taking a few moments to adjust.

He becomes aware of a presence beside him. Poppy rests her head on his shoulder, her arm wrapped around his. Nico lies at their feet. They stayed with him. Gratitude fills Theo, making his heart hurt.

Bandages cover parts of Nico's face and hands. His shirt is raised, revealing another bandage wrapped tightly around his middle. So much pain. How much destruction has Jack caused?

Theo moves his hand and Poppy sits up, suddenly alert, as if she has been waiting for that to happen for hours. People walk past but none of them look down. Poppy shakes Nico's shoulder, waking him.

They exchange looks – sad, scared, and other emotions Theo finds hard to identify. They help each other up, then walk down the hall, none of them daring to look back. They find three seats and fall into them, exhausted.

"What happened?" Theo stares at the floor, finding he can't meet their eyes.

He feels rather than sees an exchange between Poppy and Nico. He wonders at their ability to communicate silently. Will he ever know anyone well enough to do that? Poppy places her hand in Nico's and takes a deep breath.

"All the adrenaline finally hit me outside. We watched you run in screaming for help, then we came inside after you, once I'd calmed down." Poppy glanced at Nico again, as if asking whether she should continue. He gave her a nod. "We found you rocking… red and puffy with tears rolling down your face. You wouldn't let the doctors near you… muttering about it being all your fault. Nico had to go get checked, so I sat with you. You wouldn't stop so all I could do was hug you." Poppy paused, letting Nico continue for her.

"I came back, and I don't know… suddenly the floor seemed like a good place to be. You were still rocking, so we both huddled into you which seemed to calm you."

"We were like that for a few hours," Poppy added. Theo could see the exhaustion on her face.

"Well… I ended up falling asleep," Nico added. "But Poppy, she never let go of you."

Theo nods. He knows he should thank them – tell them how much they helped and how grateful he is. But somehow, that feels too overwhelming right now.

"What about Jane?" he asks instead, whispering her name.

Nico gulps, pulling at the neck of his shirt, like it's strangling him. Poppy reaches for Theo's hand and squeezes it.

"They haven't told us much but she's alive," she says. "She's alive and that's all that matters."

Theo nods, still staring at the floor.

A new pair of shoes appear in front of him. Theo's eyes look up, taking in the scrubs and ID badge.

"You three… I don't know what happened, but that doesn't matter right now. The police will need to talk to you eventually. They'll be here soon. Now you've all calmed down, I'd like your parents' names and numbers, please."

Theo's mind goes blank, but Poppy answers for him. The nurse writes down their details, including Jane's. "Her mom works in the hospital," she finishes.

The nurse looks up, horror crossing his face. "Diana's daughter…" He shakes his head, an impassive expression on his face. "You will not leave this building, understood?"

He spoke with such authority that they all nod silently, too scared to move once he walks away.

"We are so in trouble." Nico shakes his head.

"We are not in trouble. Jack is," Theo replies sourly. "All we need to do is tell the truth."

"But what if they don't believe us?" Poppy goes pale and starts to shake again.

"He'll try to deny it, but if Jane wakes up, then they'll believe us."

"Yeah, and maybe Sam and Tommy will back us up." Nico's voice is hopeful, but Theo has his doubts. They were a part of this. It's likely they will lie to save their own skins.

They sit in silence, waiting. Both Poppy and Nico's parents show up. Tears are shared, and so are hugs, as Theo watches on. His parents finally arrive. His mom looks worse for wear, as she rushes over to Theo, embracing him and telling him how sick he'd made her feel.

Theo's dad walks over slowly, his face showing a growing understanding of the situation, as he looks at the three of them.

He nods to Poppy and Nico, then wraps Theo and his mom in a hug. Unable to contain his worries, a torrent of words pours from Theo's mouth. They gently hush him, but already he feels better. Even them just being there helps. Parents can sometimes have that effect.

Across the room, the elevator doors open, and a familiar person in scrubs rushes out. Panic is written all over her face. She rushes up to the desk, asking for Jane. Her eyes scan the crowd until they land on Theo.

She walks over and Theo stands, hesitantly. Will she blame him?

The seconds grip Theo, then Jane's mom embraces him. Shocked, he takes a few steps back, before regaining his balance. His arms wrap around her, and he feels her shoulders shudder. She pulls back, holding him at arm's length. Her face is moist with tears, but she looks Theo straight in the eye.

"You saved her."

31.

Jane

Blurs of reds, whites, and blues fill Jane's vision. Darkness overcomes her, dropping her into a void before bringing her back. Flashes of fluorescent tubes race above her, blinding her. She feels a rush of wind.

A loud bang erupts from her feet, creating a new whoosh of air. She's disorientated – unsure whether she's standing or lying. Someone tugs at her shirt, and a ripping noise goes through her. There's a bustle of voices and her breathing falters. Bit by bit, everything begins to fade.

Silence drapes over her soul; a chill sprinting through her blood. The sudden coldness causes the synapses in her brain to freeze, everything coming to a standstill. She goes completely numb. Darkness wraps around her throat and she has no more willpower to fight it. All she does is wish for it to be the last time.

*

Jane wakes as if it's an emergency. She feels like she's been plunged into water. She bolts upright in the bed, her eyes alert. Sensors go off around her.

Someone beside her jumps. She tries to talk but something clogs her throat.

Reaching up, she finds a tube in her mouth. She claws at it, and nurses rush to her side pushing her down. Her mother appears beside them, face puffy and tear stained. She grabs Jane's hand and squeezes it.

Jane tries to relax but the whirlpool of doctors and nurses surrounding her makes her tense. The tube is pulled out, scratching and scouring its way up her throat to her mouth.

A coughing fit overwhelms her, forcing air in and out with each heave of her diaphragm. A nurse holds up a cup and straw to her lips. She gingerly takes a small sip before

coughing again. Slowly, her lungs relax. She lies back in the bed, tired; still holding onto her mother's hand.

The doctors and nurses' faces are flustered, bewildered, as if they didn't expect her to wake up.

"What happened?" Jane hardly recognizes her voice.

Her mom just shakes her head, tears falling. Jane looks to the doctor, pleadingly. He steps forward, shuffling his feet and clasping his hands behind his back.

"Well… Jane. May I call you Jane?"

Jane nods. He could call her Maryanne, for all she cares. She just wants to know why she's there.

"We weren't expecting you to come around so soon. You have a few serious injuries. You've just come from surgery, to reconstruct your ankle."

Flashes of images rush through her mind at the word "ankle". Jane gulps in air, trying to calm her heartrate.

"Your condition is stable, now. That's all you really need to know for the moment."

"What do you mean stable now? Was it not stable before?"

The doctor frowns, like he's debating how much to tell her. He opens his mouth, but Jane's mom lets out a sob before he can speak.

"You died Jane! For nearly three minutes."

Her words hit Jane like a physical blow. She remembers the darkness… the cold… she remembers not wanting to wake up. But her mom is still crying, and Jane can't think about that now. Losing Jane is one of her mom's biggest fears, and those three minutes must have had her at breaking point. Jane squeezes her hand, trying to pass some of the little strength she has to her mom.

"We'll let you and your mom talk. We'll be back soon if you have any questions."

"Wait!" Jane pleads.

"Yes?"

"What are my injuries? Did he… Was I…?" Jane can't seem to finish her sentence.

"Oh god…" Jane's mom drops back into her chair.

The doctor swallows but forces himself to hold Jane's eye.

"Your ankle was our biggest concern and we've done everything we can. We believe you should be walking again in a few months' time. You also have two fractured ribs and a fractured sternum. These will heal over time, but your breathing may feel constricted, and you may experience discomfort for a while. You had a number of cuts, some of which required stitches, and you should expect a significant amount of bruising."

His tone is steady, factual. It's reassuring, but he doesn't answer Jane's unspoken question.

Jane takes a few painful breaths, drawing out the few scraps of courage she has left to her.

"Did I… was I raped? I tried to fight him off, but… I just want to make sure."

Jane's mom lets out a groan. She looks like she's going to pass out. The doctor swallows again and moves closer. He sits down beside the bed, his face solemn.

"You have bruising on your thighs, which could be consistent with an assault. If you would like us to perform an internal examination, I can send in a female doctor."

Jane bites her lip to stop from crying out. Tears start to stream down her cheeks and she slowly nods yes. The doctor gives her a pitiful grimace and walks away, neither wanting to exchange any more words.

A few minutes pass before Jane can stop crying. Each sob hurts, her broken ribs crushing her lungs, but the pain is a distraction. Her mom doesn't stop crying, the wails bordering on hysteria. Jane tries to comfort her and then lets her cry – lets her get it out.

Jane lies back in the hospital bed, trying to make herself more comfortable. She notices the sheets near the bottom of her bed are propped up, a frame holding them above her broken ankle. She lifts the sheet and glances down at her foot. Metal surrounds it, holding still whatever they put inside the joint. Only then does she notice she's wearing a hospital gown and is completely naked underneath.

Gingerly, she touches her sternum and ribs. Continuing down, she feels every tender bruise under her fingertips. She chews on her lip to stop herself crying again, finishing her own examination.

Resting her hands back onto the sheets, exhaustion hits her, but sleep is the last thing she wants.

"Mom…"

Her mom looks up slowly, her eyes red and puffy.

"Mom, where are the others? Are they ok? Theo?"

Do they even know she's alive? The thought doesn't sit right with Jane.

"Yes, they're ok," her mom tells her. "They've been sitting in the waiting room since they got here. None of them want to leave – they actually refused. Nico had a few nasty cuts and a concussion, but they are all ok thankfully."

"Can I see them?"

"Yes, but I think Theo is being questioned by the police. Nico and Poppy can come in."

"What do you mean questioned?" Jane's heart breaks into a fluttering rhythm.

Her mom shakes her head. "Don't panic. It's ok. The police need to question everyone. They'll want to talk to you too when you're feeling up to it."

Jane lets out a breath she didn't know she was holding. Her brain had automatically jumped to the worst conclusion.

"I'll go get Nico and Poppy," her mom said, before leaving Jane all alone.

A few minutes later Jane hears a rush of footsteps. Poppy and Nico appear in the doorway, flustered, their smiles reaching ear to ear.

Poppy wraps her arm around Jane tightly, while Nico hovers, waiting his turn. Jane moans and Poppy retreats immediately.

"It's ok," Jane says. "I'm just sore Poppy."

Poppy tries to smile, but it comes out wobbly. She climbs up on the bed, scooting up next to Jane. Nico seems calmer and carefully hugs Jane.

"Don't ever do that to us again, Jane," Poppy says seriously.

Jane frowns. "What do you mean?"

Nico takes a seat on the edge of the bed, reaching out to hold Poppy's hand.

"You almost died!" Poppy's voice rises, and the sudden noise makes Jane flinch.

"She's ok now… It's ok," Nico says, stroking Poppy's hand. She puts an arm around Jane, and her tears dribble onto Jane's neck.

"We're all ok, thanks to you two."

Silence sits heavy around them for a moment.

"Apparently, they've already brought Jack and the others in for questioning," Poppy says.

The mention of his name makes Jane's heart drop. "Where?"

"At the police station. It's fine – there's a hospital security guard stationed outside your room, just in case," Nico says. "Nothing is going to happen to you – or any of us – again."

Jane grabs both of their hands tightly and looks back and forth between them. "Thank you. You saved me, and you didn't even think twice about it."

A knock sounds and Jane looks up. Theo stands in the doorway, his arms crossed, grinning. Nico hops up, putting his arm around Theo's shoulders, bringing him towards the bed. Jane's hands fly to her mouth, excitement and relief overwhelming her.

She never knew she could love someone like she loved Theo. Poppy and Nico exchange a knowing look.

"We'll let you two talk," Poppy says.

"But we'll be back soon," Nico adds.

Theo takes a seat on the edge of Jane's bed. He holds himself stiffly, as if he's afraid to touch her. Tears glisten in Jane's eyes, as she reaches for his hand. The contact is like a magic balm. All her worries disappear.

Theo turns away, wiping at his face. Jane moves forward, grasping his face in her hands. Seeing tears run down his

cheeks almost breaks her. Each one that slides down his face pulls another heartstring. He puts his hands over Jane's, cupping them.

"I love you," he whispers.

Millions of butterflies take a hold of Jane, making her feel like a little girl on Christmas day. "I love you too."

They close the space between them, kissing slowly at first. She feels his soft, delicate lips, like butterfly wings, kiss her back. His touch sends shivers through her body, making her tremble. He goes to stop, but she pulls him closer, not wanting it to end. He lies down on the bed next to her.

Her fists knots in his shirt, and he lets a groan roll out from deep in his throat. She breathes in his exhale. Nothing has ever felt as right as this.

His arms circle her, gathering her into him. She feels like no one else exists anymore. She doesn't know whether they've been kissing for five minutes or five hours, but she knows she doesn't want it to stop.

His leg brushes against her ankle and the kiss breaks suddenly, as she winces with pain. He darts away, moving to stand beside the bed. Jane grabs his hand, making sure he doesn't leave. The pain subsides after a few minutes, no longer demanding all of her attention.

She looks up to Theo staring at her, with the biggest puppy dog eyes she's ever seen. She starts to chuckle, though that hurts too, and her laughter becomes contagious. She pulls him back onto the bed, both of them more careful of her injuries this time. He holds her in his arms, as they continue laughing together. She has never felt safer.

## 32

Jane

Over the next few hours there are lots of visitors, and Jane is overwhelmed. Nurses come and go doing what they have to. Doctors too. Theo doesn't leave her side.

Nico and Poppy both go home with their parents but promise to come and visit once they've slept and eaten. Jane tries to persuade Theo to go home too, but he refuses. He and her mom become permanent fixtures, barely moving from their chairs by the bed.

Her mom calls Will, and he does not sound happy at all. Jane can't hear the words, but there's a lot of yelling.

The last visitors before the end of visiting hours are the police.

"Hi Miss Davidson, I'm Officer Susan and this is my colleague, Officer John. We need to speak to you alone, Miss Davidson…" the female police officer says, looking towards Theo and Jane's mother. Theo starts to protest but with a reassuring pat on the hand from Jane, he agrees to leave.

Jane is secretly relieved. She can't imagine describing everything in front of him and her mom. Theo gets up reluctantly, and so does her mom.

"We'll be right outside if you need us, love," her mom says.

Officer Susan closes the door behind them, and then takes Theo's seat. She's only a small lady but looks very mature. At least she has a friendly smile. Officer John stands at the foot of her bed, his arms crossed, looking a little awkward.

Jane waits. They seem to be holding off, as if they're afraid of what Jane might tell them. They've probably been told the same story three times from Poppy, Nico, and Theo's perspective, but perhaps hearing it from Jane – from the person it happened to – is different.

"Just tell us in your own words what happened," Officer Susan says.

Jane starts right at the beginning when Jack first grabbed her. The more she talks, the more she realizes how bad things have been. Officer John is taking notes, but she wonders if it's just an excuse not to look her in the eye.

When she finishes, Officer Susan looks nervous, as if unsure how to ask her next question.

"It's fine, whatever you're about to ask, just ask," Jane says, bluntly.

"I know this may be difficult, but I need to ask whether you were sexually assaulted, Miss Davidson."

Jane looks at her, trying to concentrate on her eyes without seeing too many flashbacks. She shakes her head, trying to clear the memories before they take hold.

"Not that I remember…" Jane trails off. She tries to answer as honestly as possible. "I can't be sure. A lot of the time I was in serious pain or knocked out, so it's hard to know. I hope not. He tried to at one point… he had his hand in my shorts, but I managed to fight him off."

Tears form in Jane's eyes. Officer Susan grabs a tissue and passes it to Jane. Officer John steps forward from the foot of the bed, clearing his throat.

"Have you had an examination? Or, um, would you consent to one?"

"The doctor asked, and I said yes, but I haven't had it yet."

He nods with a little grimace.

"Thanks for being so honest with us, Miss Davidson. Your story matches what we've heard from the other witnesses."

"I would hope so," Jane says, unable to hold back the bluntness again.

"Do you have any questions for us?" Officer John asks hesitantly. He looks like he would love to leave.

Theo hovers outside the door, and Jane motions for him to come back in. He sits next to her on the bed. "Your mom's in the restroom," he says.

"What's going to happen to them… to him?" Jane asks.

"It's too early to confirm anything, but I feel confident we'll be able to charge Jack based on your statements."

"Where is he?" Worry laces through Theo's voice.

"He's down at the station. Don't worry though, you're both safe now," the female officer says as reassuringly as she can.

Even though she knows the hospital is safe, Jane does feel better knowing Jack's behind bars.

"I think that's all, thank you," Jane says. She suddenly feels sorry for them. How many times have they had to listen to stories like hers?

Officer Susan stands. "If you think of anything that could help or if you need someone to talk to about everything, just give us a call, ok? We can put you in touch with trained counselors."

Jane nods in reply as the officers walk out the room and disappear around the corner.

Theo leans over. "Are you ok?" He gives Jane a light kiss on her bruised cheek. As he goes in for another peck, Jane's mom walks in. He changes tactics, and kisses Jane's forehead instead. This makes Jane smile, until she notices the nurse following in behind her mom.

"I'm sorry, but visiting hours are over. You need to let Jane rest. You have five minutes before I come back and have to kick you out." She smiles to show she's half-joking. Only half, though.

"I don't want to leave you," Theo says.

"It's ok," Jane says. "I'll be fine. You smell anyway."

She hears her mom snicker. "It's true, Theo. You're still covered in mud. I'll drive us home. She'll be ok, won't you, Jane?"

"I'll be fine. Besides, I've got my phone. I'll message if anything happens… which it won't!" Jane says, almost too cheerfully.

Theo sighs but leans over giving Jane a hug and a kiss. Her mom also gives her a little kiss on the cheek before they both say goodbye and walk out.

Jane hears the nurse in the corridor say a quick goodbye and reassuringly tell them, "We will take great care of her" before their footsteps continue down the hallway.

Jane hasn't been completely alone since two nights ago when she fell and thought she was going to die. Just thinking about it starts her trembling.

She tries to take some big breaths, but her ribs hurt, and all she can see is Jack charging towards her. She squeezes her eyes shut and grabs a fistful of sheet, feeling him coming closer and closer. She tells herself to breathe and forces an image of Theo into her mind.

Slowly, her breathing relaxes, easing the more she thinks of him. She releases her grip on the sheets, and lets her head fall back on the pillows, finally calm again.

Opening her eyes, she looks up at the ceiling. The lights are going out, one by one for night time. Anxiety grabs hold of her again, but she lies back, ignoring it. She turns off the bedside light, hoping to catch some much-needed sleep.

*

The doctors perform the examination early the next morning. They tell her they can't be certain about anything, but there is no evidence other than the bruising on her thighs to suggest that Jane was sexually assaulted. Jane can't hold in her tears any longer when they tell her the results. Her mom squeezes her hand tight, letting out big, heavy, relieved tears too.

Over the next few days, Jane learns to walk with crutches, only allowing herself to put the tiniest amount of pressure onto her ankle. The doctor tells her it will be at least a month before she can walk unaided.

Anytime Theo can be, he's beside her. Her mom also visits quite a bit too, which is nice. Jane knows she's juggling her nursing shifts and visiting her throughout the day.

Nico and Poppy come a couple of times, keeping her up to date with everything that's happening at school. Poppy tells her word has gotten out, and everyone can't stop talking about it.

Apparently, their geography teacher came up to Nico and Poppy and couldn't stop apologizing about what happened, even though it wasn't her fault.

Jane's glad she doesn't have to deal with the questions and the stares. School doesn't really matter anymore anyway since it's the last week. The only things left are graduation and the school dance. Jane isn't upset about missing either.

The police tell Jane they found the email address Jack created under their teacher's name and the emails he sent will be used as evidence. He was dumb enough to do it on a borrowed school laptop, so it wasn't hard to track.

His phone had been smashed during the fights, so the photos of Jane are gone, unless he has them backed up somewhere else. Even if he does, he'd be incredibly stupid to release them now. The case against Jack is looking worse and worse with every day that passes.

Will called her, telling her that he'll be coming home in around two weeks. Other than that, he just says he's glad she's ok before hanging up, nothing more.

Her last night in the hospital finally arrives. Even though she's still injured, she's thankful for her luck. She could have easily died down at the bottom of that hill, but she didn't. She could have died at Jack's hands, but she didn't. She can't wait to sleep in her own bed and eat something other than hospital food. The excitement overwhelms her, so she makes herself lie down and relax, hoping sleep will make the morning come sooner.

*

Her mom arrives at 10 a.m. on the dot, and everything has been signed off. Her mom has taken the whole day off, and Jane is looking forward to spending some time with her. They gather all of Jane's stuff, and her mom wheels her out to the car.

Jane's surprised at how nice the fresh air is. She hadn't really thought about how she has been breathing in artificial

air for the eight days she's been in hospital. She smiles at the sun that had come out to greet her. Summer is finally here.

Slowly, she gets herself comfortable in the car before they set off.

Theo is waiting on their front porch. He bounds down the steps, arriving at her car door in seconds. He helps her up, almost picking her up.

Jane shakes her head. "I want to practice with my crutches." She can't be carried everywhere, she thinks.

Theo and her mom both hover close by, ready to catch her at any moment, but Jane makes it up the stairs and inside – albeit slowly.

Inside, Jane is blown away by the number of gifts people have sent. She starts to laugh. At one point, she thought no one cared about her, but now realizes, she was wrong.

She looks at Theo, who seems uncomfortable with everything around him, and that makes her laugh more. It must be the drugs, she thinks. Everything seems funny when painkillers are involved.

All three of them sit on the couch together, eating popcorn and snacks, while watching a movie. She's tired when it finishes, so begins the trek upstairs to her room. Theo cautiously walks right behind her, and her mom goes up the stairs backwards in front of her. For now, the hovering is fine Jane thinks, but eventually, they will have to give her space.

At the top, she takes a few crutch-aided steps towards her room. Her door is already open, and before she even steps inside, a floral scent drifts out to greet her. She glances at Theo who looks down sheepishly. A smile spreads across her lips.

Vases and vases of different flowers line her room. Almost every corner is filled with blossoms. Speechless, she turns on the spot, taking in the different flowers. She limps around the room, touching the petals, and breathing in the perfumes.

She looks towards the doorway. Theo and her mom stand watching her.

"I'll leave you two love birds alone," her mom says. "Call me if you need anything, hun."

Jane and Theo both watch her go. Theo picks up a purple anemone, bringing it over to Jane. Her smile broadens. She feels like the luckiest girl on earth.

"Theodore Gray Williams, did you really do this all for me?"

"Of course, I did, Jane Lilibet Davidson."

"I didn't know you knew my middle name."

"And I didn't know you knew mine…"

They both start to laugh again and slowly sit down on Jane's bed. He touches Jane's hand, turning it over and kissing it, smiling against it.

"Why all the flowers?" Jane asks.

Theo looks shy. "Well… I wanted to bring our garden to you, so we could still do what we planned on doing all summer."

Jane's heart melts, realizing how much effort he must have gone through to set all this up.

"I love you, Theo, more than my words can express. You are my everything," she says, meaning every word.

"And you are mine." He leans his forehead onto hers.

## 33

Theo

Theo wakes to his alarm going off. It's 9 a.m. Groggily, he drags his hand out from under his sheets, hitting it down on his bedside table until it makes contact with his clock. It slips off the table and lands on the ground next to his bed. This almost changes his mood, but then he remembers Jane is right next door.

She's been home for three days now. Theo's barely left her side, except to come home to sleep. Mostly, they've just chilled in her room, looking at the portable garden he made for her. It was the only thing that had kept him sane while she was in the hospital. Otherwise, his thoughts would have consumed him.

Slowly, he pushes himself up in bed, twisting around and letting his feet touch the floor. Resting his elbows on his knees, he rubs at his eyes, still trying to wake himself up. He stares down at his clock and the other things he knocked off in the process of trying to silence the alarm.

He replaces the clock and starts tidying up the rest of the mess. Three envelopes lie in the middle of it – apology letters.

They'd been sitting on Jane's bed when he started making her the garden. Her mom must have put them there for her to read when she was ready, but Theo didn't think she would ever be ready, especially since one was from Jack.

Theo wasn't quite sure why Sam, Tommy, and Jack had written Jane apology letters, but no doubt the police had made them do it as some sort of "therapy".

Theo would eventually give them to Jane, but it was still too soon.

Placing them in his drawer one by one, Jack's letter is the last to go in. Theo holds it out in front of him. Turning it over, he slides his thumb underneath the seal, slowly breaking it. It feels like a ticking time bomb waiting to go off in his face once the seal is completely broken.

The letter is only one line long. This makes Theo even more nervous. Unfolding it, he takes a deep breath in, his eyes pouncing on the words in front of him. He shudders, unable to stop himself reading Jack's words over and over.

*I don't regret what I've done but you will.*

Emotions flood through Theo and suddenly it's hard to breathe. Everything overwhelms him and the only thing he seems to grasp onto is rage. He leaps up, running downstairs with the letter in his hand. He grabs the lighter from above the fireplace and runs the edge of the letter over the flame. It lights immediately and the fire eats up Jack's words, erasing them.

The flame puts Theo into a sort of trance. The kitchen screen door opens, hitting the doorstop behind it, the noise startling him. He throws the letter into the fireplace and puts the lighter down as fast as he can.

There's no movement from the kitchen. Both of his parents are out. Today is his dad's last chemo session – no one should be home. He grabs the fire poker, and slowly makes his way towards the kitchen.

Quietly turning the corner, the kitchen's empty. Did the wind blow the door open?

He unhooks the door to close it, but movement out in his garden catches his eye. He clutches the poker, and takes the steps outside one by one, trying to be as quiet as he can. His heart thuds in his ears with every step closer to the trespasser. He crouches behind a hedge and slowly peeks around the corner.

It's Jane. Her back is to him, but she looks gorgeous in a summer dress. Her hair moves in the wind, and the hem of her dress flows with it.

Theo drops the poker under the hedge and stands up, not wanting to startle her. She still hasn't noticed him. She moves carefully over to the butterfly bush filled with blooming flowers. Reaching out her hand, she lets a butterfly walk onto

her finger and slowly but surely, she raises it to her face to get a closer look, as if she's about to kiss it.

Theo feels himself fall completely in love with her all over again. Jack's letter is gone, no longer a thought in his mind. He's now completely consumed by Jane.

She has this new light radiating off her. She spins around with her crutches, as delicately as she can, coming face to face with him. She smiles, making him feel giddy. She opens her arms, encouraging a hug and she looks as free as a butterfly in the sanctuary they've made. Theo closes the space between them, embracing her and spinning them both around. He can't take his eyes off her, as he slows to a stop. He sees all of her, the joy and sorrow, and knows at that very moment that he is going to marry this girl.

What a journey this book has taken us on… If you're reading this now and are too scared to speak out about how you're feeling or what has happened to you just like Jane was, please, don't be.

Helplines you can call:

**NEW ZEALAND**
Sexual Harm Helpline: 0800 044334
Text: 4334

Youth Line Helpline: 0800 376 633
Free text: 234

Need to Talk Helpline: 1737 for mental health support from
a trained counselor.
Free text: 1737

The Lowdown Helpline text: 5626, straight up answers and
help for when 'life sucks'.

Grief and Loss Helpline: 0800 611 116

**AUSTRALIA**
1800 Respect (abuse) Helpline: 1800 737 732

Lifeline Helpline: 13 11 14

Beyond Blue Helpline: 1300 224 636

Grief and Loss Helpline: 13 11 14 – 24

**UNITED STATES**
National Sexual Assault Hotline: 1 800 656 HOPE (4673)

Stop it Now: 1 888 PREVENT

Youth Crisis Hotline: 1 800 448 4663

Teen Hope Line: 1 800 394 HOPE

Griefshare: 1 800 395 5755

If these helplines don't apply to you, please google your national helpline. It's ok to reach out for help, to talk. You are not being a burden.

*Remember, you're valued, you're strong, and you are irreplaceable.*

# ACKNOWLEDGMENTS

I'd like to give my warmest thanks to everyone who has helped me make this book happen –

**Helen Fletcher** – has been the BEST editor and so much more. Honestly, I'm not sure whether this book would've been published without her help. She has been more than an editor to me. I'd like to say that Helen would be my friend and my teacher, that I'm yet to meet! Helen guided me through all areas of self-publishing. She was a shoulder to lean on who always offered her help throughout the whole process. I cannot wait to work on the next project with her!

**Olivia Peterson** – for taking on my project that I would call "My Brain". Olivia brought my very complicated thoughts to life. She unscrambled them and made a book cover that I ABSOLUTELY adore! AND helped me with the formatting. Olivia is the best sister I could ever ask for.

**Kelsey Flynn** – for doing my first proof read!

**Victoria Peterson** – my amazing mother, by using her puzzling brain to do my second proof read! Thanks for being patient with me, I couldn't have asked for a better mother!

**Victoria McPherson** – for doing my final proof read! You made me feel confident that everything was correct before going ahead with printing. I can't thank you enough for all your help!

**Monroe Brackey & Megan Moreno** – for making sure I wasn't culturally insensitive in anyway, in your readers report. Also, for making me feel confident in what I was about to publish!

My family and friends - they motivated me and pushed me to keep going on the hardest days. Thank you for always being excited with me.

Lastly, I would like to thank every single one of you for reading my book! I wish I could give you the BIGGEST hug, and I wish I could hear every thought you've had about my

book. Thank you for giving "The Butterfly Sanctuary" a go, and welcome to the *butterfly* family.

I would LOVE to hear your thoughts! Please share them by leaving your review on the site you purchased my book or my Instagram page (@grp.books)!

You can also contact me by sending me an email at grp.books.co@gmail.com

Thanks!

www.ingramcontent.com/pod-product-compliance
Lightning Source LLC
Chambersburg PA
CBHW032008050726
47590CB00006B/2096